WHEN THE CARDINAL CALLS

Tim Maceyko

SJ the Monkey Press
P.O. Box 136
Cardington, Ohio 43315

Publication Year: 2019

This book is dedicated to Seth James Maceyko.

His smile made this world a brighter place

and his memory will live forever.

◆ ◆ ◆

And In Memory Of

*My father Tom Maceyko, my wife's mother
Mable Elkins and the many others who
we have lost along the way.*

"Why is it so hard to believe that our loved ones can reach out to us after they die? If it's not them then, at the very least, it's God allowing us to know that they are OK. Either way, I now find comfort whenever I hear the cardinal call."

- Tim Maceyko

SJ the Monkey Press
P.O. Box 136
Cardington, Ohio 43315

Ordering Information:
Quantity sales. Special discounts are available on quantity purchases by corporations, associations, and others. For details, contact the publisher at the address above or email: timmaceyko@ gmail.com.

Orders by U.S. trade bookstores and wholesalers. Please email: timmaceyko@gmail.com.

Printed in the United States of America: First Edition

CHAPTER ONE

How Was Your Day?

The emergency room was a circus, with nurses rushing all around the small area. They were barking out orders, hooking up things, and moving around the room as quickly as they could. I stood at full attention in the background, quietly analyzing the situation.

Everyone was frantically working to save my five-year-old son, and I could do nothing but just stand there and watch. A father is supposed to protect his children, save them from bad situations, and make things right when they go wrong. However, in that moment I could do nothing but observe - and it was the most helpless feeling I'd ever had.

Someone yelled out, "Life Flight is here!" as two medics in flight gear walked in the room.Knowing the Life Flight helicopter was on stand-by, ready to go filled me with an immense sense of hope. It also instilled in me more than just a bit of fear. I was afraid their being there meant my child's injury was even more serious than I may have realized; yet, I was still hopeful because I knew they could get Seth down to Children's Hospital in Columbus as quickly as possible, once he was stabilized.

Suddenly and unexpectedly, the doctor who'd been directing everything stopped and turned to me. I'll never forget what she said to me that day. I'd heard the words she spoke before, in the movies, on television shows - yet until that very moment, I'd always thought they were simply made up for dramatic effect.

I'm guessing you've heard these words before, too. She looked me in the eyes that day, and in a soft, gentle tone she said, "I'm sorry. We did everything we could."

And just like that, Seth was gone.

The room cleared out quickly, and I was suddenly all alone. All the noise I'd heard just seconds ago was gone, and now there was nothing but silence.

Where did Life Flight go? Is this how it's

supposed to end? What about my wife? How is she going to handle this?

The day had started off so normal. That morning, the alarm on my phone went off at 7:00 AM, like every other day. I slowly rolled out of bed and made my way to the bathroom. I took my shower. I brushed my teeth. I shaved and did all the typical good hygiene things a person is supposed to do. In fact, it was the same routine I followed every morning.

I walked down the hall and into my son's bedroom and announced it was time to get up. Seth groaned and pulled up the covers over his head.

"I'm not going," he stubbornly announced.

"Oh yes, you are," I replied matter-of-factly. Seth whimpered a little and remained steadfast in his goal of remaining comfortable in his bed. "You have five minutes to get dressed, young man," I announced in a stern voice.

We had a regular morning routine, and my son's refusal to get out of bed on this particular morning was going to put that routine in jeopardy. I usually didn't allow for a lot of extra time in the mornings, because neither Seth nor I were exactly good morning people. My wife, Trish, seemed comfortable enough getting up early, but for me and my son, it was quite a chore to say the least.

Most mornings, Trish would get up earlier than both of us and be out the door for work well before my alarm went off; this left me alone with the early morning duties of getting our little one up and off to the sitter on workdays. I didn't actually mind this responsibility, as it gave me a few minutes each morning to spend with my son - but honestly, neither of us was initially in the mood to enjoy each other's company when we first woke.

The routine itself was easy enough, because Seth would typically eat breakfast at the sitter's house. Not having to worry about that allowed me to let him sleep in until the last possible minute, thus avoiding too early of a wake-up call and an unreasonably crabby child. The only drawback to that philosophy? On mornings when Seth didn't want to get up, we didn't have a lot of time to negotiate.

After making repeated requests for Seth

to get out of bed, and getting his outright refusal in return, I finally played the parent card. You know the one, where you use *that* voice. The one your parents used with you when you were younger.

"You're going to make me late, young man," I announced in a deeper tone. "I'm going to start the truck, and you better be out of that bed when I walk back in, or else."

I've always appreciated the "or else" part of that statement. Or else what? I'm not sure even I knew what the "or else" would actually involve, but it sure seemed like the perfect thing to add to my statement for extra effect.

I exited the room and proceeded out the front door to warm up the truck. Rather than continue to argue with a five-year-old, I figured I'd just move on to the next thing that needed to be done. If you've ever had the privilege of arguing with a young child, I'm sure you understand my logic quite well.

I started the truck, then went back inside the house. I was busy gathering things in the kitchen when Seth walked around the corner. He was dressed, shoes on, coat on, and he had a big smile on his face.

"I'm ready, Dad," he announced as he literally jumped around the corner and landed in a pose, proudly showing off how he was fully dressed and ready to go.

"Seth was one of those good looking kids with bright blue eyes and sandy blond hair. At just five years of age, he was already far better looking than I ever hoped to be. Girls were drawn to him whenever he flashed that smile, and he knew exactly how to ham it up when necessary. So on this morning when he flashed that smile and added, "I was just kidding" in his most playful voice, my heart melted, and I felt a twinge of guilt for using my dad voice earlier. "I was just kidding" was the phrase Seth utilized whenever he thought I was mad at him. It was his way of letting me know he understood and didn't want to upset me.

Actually, I wasn't mad at him at all. I just knew we were going to be running late if I was unable to get him moving, so maybe saying I was a little irritated is a fair way to describe my mood in this case, but I certainly wasn't mad at him.

"I know, little buddy" I replied. "You're the best."

With that, Seth flashed that big smile

one more time, and life was better. It's funny how a child's smile always seems to make everything better. I can't explain it; it just does. So, I scooped him up and gave him a big hug as we headed out the door.

The drive to the babysitter's house was a short three minutes and forty-nine seconds, and as I backed up the vehicle to leave our driveway, Seth asked me to put on his song. I had to laugh. It seemed like every single morning, Seth would ask me to put on that song. It was a beautiful, slow, country song by an artist named Billy Currington entitled "Let Me Down Easy."

I'm not sure exactly why, but Seth absolutely loved that song, and he would sit in the back seat and sing along word-for-word. I would listen as I heard his little voice sing, "If I fall, will you let me down easy?" The song would typically end right as we got to the sitter's house. Even today, I still believe it was the most enjoyable three minute and forty-nine second drive a person could possibly have.

After we arrived at our destination, I carried Seth in, sat him down in the doorway, and helped him remove his coat. I then gave him another hug, told him I loved him, and not wanting to be late for work, quickly headed back out the door.

I've thought about that morning over and over since then. I've re-lived it many times in my mind and replayed every word Seth and I said to each other that day. Every action, every facial expression, everything. There's nothing specific that stands out in a negative way, but I wish I hadn't felt so rushed that particular morning. I wish we could have enjoyed that time a little more, and I wish I could go back and do it all over again.

My workday would typically end by about 4:00 PM, but I also coached junior high girls' basketball, so during the season my days would be much longer. I would often need to head straight to the gym after my regular job, and on those days it was normal for me to pick up Seth and take him to practice with me. There weren't many days when my son wasn't right by my side in the morning before work, then right there again after work.

When basketball season was over, I would make it a point to try to be home for dinner. I truly cherished it when we had the chance to sit around the dining room table as a family and talk, which was a rare occurrence between the months of October and March. With coaching and my daughter, Allie, very involved in sports herself, it was always a constant struggle to find time together as a family.

As many of you know, it can be extremely difficult to get everyone around the table to sit and eat together once extra-curricular activities begin. I know that's the case for most families, good or bad.

So, during the months I wasn't coaching, we did try to get in more of those family dinners, and during those dinners, it always seemed to be Seth who would initiate the conversation first. As we'd all sit down in our chairs around the dining room table, it would be Seth who would look at his mother and say, "So Mom, how was your day?" He would then stare intently at her and wait patiently for her response.

Trish would tell him about work and what she did that particular day, and he would listen as if his mommy's words were the most important thing in the world. Then he'd go around the table and ask his sister how her day was, then it would be my turn. If we were lucky enough to have Seth's older brother Connor, who had moved out previously, visit for dinner, Seth would ask him the same thing.

It always amazed me how such a young little boy could bring so much light to a room. He knew how to make you feel special, and he brought nothing but love to our lives. He cherished who you were as a person, and he always wanted to hear what you had to say, regardless of what you were actually saying. Those family dinners were an opportunity for us just to be together, and they proved to be some of the best, most special moments of my entire life.

On this particular day though, I failed to make it home for dinner that evening. I had to attend a late meeting, then, upon returning to the office, I had a few last-minute things to address before heading home. It was well after 6:00 PM when I last glanced at the clock.

Since Seth's birth, I'd never stayed at the office that late, but for some reason things weren't working out for me that day. As I stood there talking with a co-worker, my phone rang; it was my wife. I figured she was calling to ask me why I was so late and if I was ever coming home; however, when I answered her call, I never expected to hear the things I heard that day.

My wife was frantic. She was screaming at me, and I could hardly make out what she was saying. She was hysterical, and I did my best to get her to calm down, explaining that I couldn't understand her.

I had no idea what could make my wife so out of sorts, but I was finally able to make out the words, "Tim, come home."

Her breathing was abnormal, and the pure terror I could hear in her voice shook me to the core as I heard her repeat, "Tim, come home."

That was all she could get out, and that was more than enough for me to know what I needed to do. I turned and sprinted out the door.

In all the years I'd known my wife, I'd never heard that kind of desperation before. The fear of what may be going on consumed me more than I can explain. It was easily the most frightening moment of my entire life so far.

I work in a small rural community, and my office is very close to my home, so as soon as I emerged from the building, I could hear the sirens. My heart sank and my stomach flipped, as I somehow knew those sirens were meant for my house. I instantly became sick.

I jumped into my truck and sped out of the company parking lot. I felt the vehicle fish-tail onto the main road, and I knew I was driving unsafely, but I couldn't help it. My safety meant nothing to me at that moment. Something was seriously wrong, and I needed to travel those few miles home as fast as I could. I can't even recall the specific details of my drive that day, but I know it felt like it took forever to get there.

CHAPTER TWO

We Can Pray and Hope

As I raced home, my mind began trying to figure out the possibilities of what was actually going on. I naturally tend to be the kind of person who has a need to reason and deduce things in some sort of a logical manner, and I like to approach things from more of a scientific mindset. In that terrifying moment, I was still trying to determine logically what I may be facing, and I tried to line up what I did know first.

Because of her schedule, my daughter shouldn't be home, so this couldn't be about her. My wife had called me, so I knew the emergency wasn't about her either. That left only two options. First, there were the dogs, Princess and Annie. I quickly rationalized there wouldn't be sirens or such a state of panic for the dogs. I mean, sure, they're a dear part of our family, but our pets wouldn't be cause for such an alarm.

That left only one other logical option, and it wasn't an option I was willing to consider. There must be something I was missing. There had to be another reason, something I just wasn't thinking of. My mind refused to accept the possibility that our five-year old son may be the reason for all of this.

As I pulled up the driveway, I noticed multiple police cars, an ambulance, and several other vehicles already there. I maneuvered around the cars and emergency vehicles and veered into the yard. I barely had the truck in park before I leapt out and ran towards the front door. Someone told me to stop, but I heard another voice say, "He's the father" as I bolted through the front door.

Needless to say, I wasn't prepared for what I saw that day. Lying there on the floor in the dining room was my son, surrounded by the paramedics. He seemed even smaller than he was with those big bodies hovering over top of him. Seth didn't appear to be moving, and I froze at the sight. They were performing CPR on him as my wife sat at the dining room table, staring at the scene in front of her with a blank look on her face.

Realizing I couldn't do anything for my son at that moment, I went to my wife and ushered her out of the room; this wasn't something she needed to be watching. As I tried to comfort her, I also tried to figure out what had occurred. Trish was in a complete state of shock, but she did manage to tell me bits and pieces of what had happened. After that, I was able to figure out the rest on my own.

Trish had picked up Seth from the babysitter, and knowing I was going to have a longer than normal day, she took him to McDonalds for dinner. They got their food through the drive-thru, and upon returning home, Seth had told his mom he wanted to go play in his room. When Trish pressed him about eating his dinner, he told her he wanted to wait until his daddy got home so we could all eat together. With that, he went off to play.

Seth loved to play in his bedroom whenever it was about time for me to come home. His bedroom window faced the driveway, so Seth would hear me pull up. It was normal for me to see his cute little face pressed against the window or his head pop up into view from behind the curtain whenever I pulled in. So, him playing in his room today was no different in that regard, yet today was very different.

After not hearing anything from Seth for a while, my wife got curious. Her first thought was that the silence might mean he fell asleep, but it was entirely too late in the day for him to be taking a nap. This train of thought naturally caused her to walk down the hallway and into Seth's room.

When she opened his door, what Trish encountered was something no parent would ever expect to see. It was something no parent should ever *have* to see. I find it difficult to write about it. It's just too hard to try to describe, even now.

I spent a lot of time trying to figure out a way to explain to you what had occurred without making it seem too graphic, but there really is no way to sugarcoat it. There's no way to make the tragedy seem like less than what it was. It was horrifying in every way imaginable.

According to Nationwide Children's Hospital, there are more than 36,000 injuries to children each year that are the direct result of bunk bed usage. Who would have guessed the number would be that high?

Through 1999, there were no bunk bed specification requirements; only voluntary recommendations, and the lax regulations for manufacturers allowed the market to be flooded with dangerously designed products, unbeknownst to the majority of the public. Ann Brown, the CPSC Chairman in 2000, stated, "I voted today to issue a final rule to require bunk bed manufacturers to make bunk beds that will not entrap and strangle young children. About ten children die every year due to entrapment on bunk beds that do not meet current voluntary safety standards."

The CPSC issued 630,000 recalls after their

new requirements went into effect because many manufacturers continued to disregard them. I share all of that with you because the bed we had in our family was manufactured around 1999-2000 and failed those new safety standards.

Unfortunately, we never understood the extent of the danger that existed in our own home, so when my wife walked into our son's room on that day in March 2013, there was no way she could have expected to find what she did: Seth, entangled and in duress.

I cringed when I later heard the 9-1-1 call. It made me queasy to listen to my wife's voice as she screamed for help. I was beyond mortified when I imagined how she must have felt as she tried to perform CPR on our child, all by herself, waiting desperately for help to come. No parent should have to face something as terrifying as what she did, and the fact that she had to face it all alone still brings tears to my eyes whenever I think about it.

After having a little understanding of what seemed to have occurred, I rushed back in to check on how my son was doing. I wanted to know if the paramedics were making any progress, but when I returned to the dining room area, I found they'd already loaded Seth into the ambulance and were heading to the hospital.

I certainly wasn't thinking clearly at that point

in time, but I remember telling my wife I'd call her as I rushed out the door to follow the ambulance. One of the sheriff's deputies on the scene knew me personally and refused to allow me to drive.

I initially resisted his efforts to keep me from my vehicle, but he was firm in his stance. Of course, I was firm in my position that I was going to get to the hospital - immediately. This is basically my polite way of explaining to you that I was arguing with a police officer, something I typically never would condone.

Finally, realizing time was being wasted by useless pleas, I relented and accepted the offered transport. I truly didn't want anyone to drive me, as I didn't think there was any reason, but I knew I had little choice if I wanted to get to the hospital. It was with that understanding I entered the passenger's seat of the sheriff's car.

The officer who ended up driving me to the hospital that day was someone I didn't personally know, and as we drove along, all I could think about was how I wished he would drive a lot faster.

Why doesn't he just turn on the siren and go about ninety miles per hour? I bet he'd go a lot faster if it was his child, I thought.

I once again began rationalizing the situation in my head. My wife had called 9-1-1 and performed CPR, so that was good. She'd said Seth had thrown up, so that seemed like it might be a good sign. I realized I was talking about these things out loud when the officer glanced my way.

His eyes told me maybe things were worse than my mind was allowing me to think they were. As he continued to drive along silently, he just listened to the things I was saying without saying a word - but those eyes...they told a different story; they said I should prepare for the worst.

Seeing his expressions, I decided to question him directly. Maybe I was reading him wrong. Maybe he would tell me everything was fine and my fear was just an overreaction.

It was with that thought in mind I asked the officer, "He threw up, so that's a good thing, right?"

The officer looked directly at me and said, "We can pray and hope."

But those eyes. Those eyes. They said something much different.

CHAPTER THREE

An Unexpected Storm

I finally arrived at the emergency room at the local hospital, and after a brief wait in the lobby, I was ushered into a room where Seth was. As I described earlier, things were crazy and people were frantic in their efforts to save my child, but it was simply not meant to be.

After hearing the doctor say, "I'm sorry. We did everything we could," my world became a blur. I felt light-headed and dizzy. This wasn't right. It wasn't real. I heard the doctor's voice again, and I wasn't sure what she was saying until I heard, "I want you to hold your son's hand and be with him."

I approached the bed and looked down at my child. Nothing actually looked wrong with him; he was still the same beautiful little boy he'd always been. At first, I held his hand and just stared at him. None of this was registering. My brain refused to accept it. The doctor had to be wrong.

I could still do something, couldn't I? I glanced around the room. I looked back into the hallway, expecting someone to come back, but the staff was quietly going about their business. No one was paying me any attention, and I didn't know what to do.

Finally understanding everyone had given up, I took Seth in my arms. I picked him up off the bed and held him tight. I'll never forget how that moment made me feel. I'm not sure I can even put it into words, but my heart was full of love for my son, and yet I was cold, too. So cold. For the first time since this all started, I began to cry.

Soon, I was sobbing as I held him this last time, not knowing how I was going to go on after this. How was I going to be strong for everyone else when I was now broken? My mind raced, my feelings overwhelmed me, and my heart tore apart. I was no longer the person I'd been. In this moment, everything I was changed. The very essence of who I'd been my entire life had just been altered. I would never see the world the same way again. Everything was changed, forever.

Eventually, I regained my composure and realized I was still alone. Trish hadn't yet made her way to the hospital, so I called her. It turned out she was still at the house. She'd been evaluated medically herself, answered some questions, and was preparing to make her way to the hospital.

Can you imagine having to be the one who makes that phone call? To tell your spouse your child didn't make it? That her baby was gone? I dreaded the idea of even trying to find the words.

I took a deep breath and just laid it out there. I don't even remember my exact words anymore. I don't know if I was compassionate enough with my delivery, or if I was supportive enough. All I know is, I had to stand there and tell my wife on the phone our son was gone. You can probably imagine her reaction, and you're probably right. That was the single worst phone call of my life, but it wasn't going to be the last.

My daughter had already been alerted that something was wrong and I was at the hospital with Seth. I felt I needed to be the one to call her and talk to her about everything, although I wasn't sure what I would say. What do you do in a situation like that? How do you tell your daughter, on the phone, her little brother had died? Do you let her come to the hospital and then tell her? Do you not say anything and have her stay where she is?

My mind was reeling not knowing how to handle the call. It all went better than anticipated though, as the word was already getting around and Allie had heard more about what was going on than I expected. Her voice shook and trembled as she tried to respond to what I was telling her. She took it as well as someone could under those circumstances, but it was another difficult call nonetheless.

Then I began to think about who all needed to be called. My mom knew what was going on, so she'd be able to alert my brother, sister, and my side of the family. I wasn't sure if Trish was mentally in a place where she could tell her family, but at the time I didn't have phone numbers in my phone for my wife's side of the family, so I was unable to call them myself. I just hoped someone would be letting them know.

I especially wanted to be sure my step-son, Connor, was informed since he didn't live with us at the time. Connor had recently reached his twenties and was busy doing what many young boys do at that age, out trying to find his own way, so he wasn't around as much these days. *He had to be told.*

These were the things that were quickly and abruptly going through my mind. I then thought of someone whose number I did have, so I made a call to a young man named Cameron Phelps.

I'd coached Cameron in Little League Baseball, and, initially, he began staying at the house because he was the same age as Connor, but as the years passed, Cameron became like one of our own kids. He would come over to visit and stay even when Connor wasn't with us. Cameron became another big brother to Allie and Seth. In fact, Cameron had been there for Seth's entire life. He was literally a big part of our family, so at that moment I wanted to be the one to tell him what had occurred.

When Cameron answered my call, I wasted little time getting to the point. "Cameron, Seth died," I blurted out.

"What? Seth got hurt?" was Cameron's response.

I knew he'd heard me, and I knew he simply didn't want it to be true. I repeated myself a second time, "Seth died."

There was a brief pause on the other end of the phone before I heard Cameron speak again. His voice was shaking as he tried to talk, and I could tell his tears were beginning to flow. I told him I understood and asked him to let his family know. I told him I'd get back with him later, then we hung up.

After ending my call with Cameron, I then went into my own state of shock of sorts. I stood there patiently waiting for my wife, mom, and daughter to arrive at the hospital, and I felt very alone. Sheriff Steve Brenneman had arrived at the hospital, and although I knew he was there in an official capacity, I also knew Steve to be a strong, upstanding Christian, and he lent me a shoulder to cry on in that moment. He also gave me encouraging words, and something about his presence gave me comfort.

God puts people in our path at times when we need it, and in that moment it was Sheriff Brenneman who was meant to be there - and I was thankful for that.

After my brief breakdown, I gathered myself back together and once again began going through the contacts list on my phone, wondering if there was anyone else I needed to call. As I came across a friend's name, Troy Ruehrmund, something deep down urged me to call him. So, I did.

Troy was on the local youth baseball board at the time, and the two of us went way back. He was just a few years younger than me, and we'd gone to school together and known each other most of our lives. We'd coached both with each other and against each other on the ball fields over the years, so he also knew my family well; as such, he knew Seth well.

For this year's upcoming baseball season, I'd signed up to coach Seth's t-ball team, so in my unusual state of mind, I'd decided I needed to, at that very moment, tell Troy I'd be unable to coach the team.

When he answered his phone, I almost shouted, "Troy, this is Tim Maceyko, and I wanted you to know I can't coach the t-ball team this year. Seth died." There, that was simple enough.

I can't imagine what Troy was thinking to hear such a thing. His reply was pretty much what you'd expect upon hearing something so crazy. "What? Where are you?" he asked.

When I told him I was at the hospital and repeated what I'd said about Seth, he asked if he could come be with me, which I appreciated. Soon enough, Troy was standing at my side.

As it turned out, Troy would be standing by my side from that moment on as I struggled to come to terms with this new life I needed to face. They say we're guided to the people and places we need, whenever we need them, and I believe that's true.

I certainly didn't have a truly good reason to call Troy that day, but something told me to make that call, as weird as it must have seemed at the time. Troy had no obligation to me and could have simply offered his sympathy and gone on with his own life. He didn't have to make the offer to come be at my side that night, but he did, and he's been there ever since.

My wife and mother had finally arrived at the hospital. I won't share the intimate details of those moments because they're theirs to share or keep for themselves. What I will say is, the emotion, pain, and tears I witnessed that night were downright overbearing; even writing about it now causes me to tear up yet again.

So many people came and went while we were there at the hospital that evening. I know Trish's sisters and father were there, several of my aunts and uncles, a few friends, and both Allie and Connor made it. To be honest, I'm not even sure who all was actually there, what they said, or how long we all stayed. My mind was a mess.

Due to my stubborn refusal to leave the hospital until they came and took Seth, we ended up being there for quite some time, but I'd made up my mind: I was staying at my son's side as long as I could. Something seemed wrong about leaving him there all alone. I just couldn't do it. I wouldn't do it. Once the paramedics finally arrived and took him out to be transported, I felt like then, and only then, could I go.

As they were taking Seth out of the back doors of the hospital, it began to snow. It started as a light snow, but by the time we were prepared to leave ourselves and load into Troy's vehicle for our drive, the snow had worked itself up into a frenzy and was coming down in huge flakes at a rapid pace.

Soon we could barely see anything at all, and we were all surprised by this burst of severe weather. None of us had seen a weather report that had called for anything this significant! It seemed highly unusual to us at the time, but it was March in Ohio.

Because Trish couldn't bear the idea of going back home, we'd all come to the conclusion that my mom's house made the most sense as the place for us to stay for the next few days. Her home was still local and just a few minutes from our own, so Troy was driving us there as the snow kept falling. The snow continued to pick up in intensity, and soon it was almost blizzard-like conditions.

We were all surprised even more before that drive was over, because at the very moment that we pulled up to my mom's house the snow quit. It didn't taper off or slow down. It just completely quit.

It had started exactly as Seth was leaving the hospital. It picked up in severity as we drove away, then literally stopped right when we reached our destination. The intensity had magnified, much like our emotions at the time, then it was just over. Just gone.

Comments were made about it being Seth's tears from Heaven and maybe the snow was Seth's message to us. I'm not sure it really mattered what it was, but it gave us a little light that night after our entire world had suddenly been filled with darkness.

CHAPTER FOUR

Snuggle Time

The next several days were a whirlwind. They were filled with visits from family, friends, and people wanting to show their love and support. There were lots of hugs, tears, and so much emotion, by the time the late evening rolled around, I was emotionally drained.

When people asked me how I was doing, I responded by saying, "The world's dark. That's what happens when God takes away your sunshine. I was numb and angry.

The tears flowed freely, and I was still expecting my son to walk through the door. On the one hand I knew Seth was gone, but on the other I was having difficulty believing it. My mind just didn't want to process or accept this reality. So, in certain ways, it didn't.

Everything was wrong, and I could only imagine

how much worse it was for my wife. Knowing what she'd gone through and how the night terrors were keeping her awake only added to my own pain. Watching my mother cry, knowing that she had already suffered so much through other losses made this seem even more unfair for her.

My daughter was suffering as well, and her tears were painful to see. It was frustrating knowing I couldn't help any of the women in my life. There was no way to ease their pain or truly comfort them. I didn't have the strength, words, or answers.

It was the most helpless feeling I'd ever experienced. However, I also knew I was going to have to rise up and find the strength to lead my family through this difficult time. I just wasn't sure I could do it.

The one thing I was sure of though was the love that was being shown. I cannot speak highly enough about the support our family, friends, and the entire community showed. Unlimited sympathy cards were coming in, words of encouragement and donations for Seth's memorial fund poured in, and people were constantly bringing food.

Family and friends were spending their entire day with us. People were coming and going constantly, and the love we felt from others was literally keeping us afloat.

One day, Kianna, a young lady I'd coached years earlier, stopped by with her mother and father. Her dad told me even though she didn't really know Seth, she'd never forgotten how much I'd helped her during her junior high years. As soon as she knew I was hurting, she'd told him she had to stop, so there they were.

Kianna had been an amazing athlete at a young age and gone on to have a lot of success, even playing college basketball. So, standing there that day, knowing I'd impacted her in such a positive way, that she now felt the need to be there for me, meant so much. They didn't stay long, as Kianna was heading back to school. As I recall, she didn't say much, but no words were needed; her mere presence said everything.

I'm amazed at how great the human spirit can be when people decide to rally around something; for that, I'm grateful more than words can express. Yet despite all the support and love sent our way, I was still in a bad place mentally. My brain just wouldn't work like it did in the past.

I couldn't watch a television show or ball game because I was simply unable to focus for any length of time. I needed shorter conversations that changed topics often for me to participate. Anything that required much thought lost me.

I didn't mention any of these things to others, but I knew my mind was in a different place, and it was rather scary. The fact that I couldn't think coherently was pretty frightening, actually. Eventually, it corrected itself, but the stress of the experience was traumatizing in more ways than even I realized.

Normally by midnight, the visits would stop, the relatives would go home, and my wife, daughter, and mom would all go to bed. I'd then be left alone to sit in the living room and think.

The first night, I'd tried to lay down with my wife, but I couldn't do it. I just couldn't sleep, nor did I want to. As much my wife needed me, I couldn't provide that comfort to her when the night came. Thankfully, her sister would stay with her while I dealt with things my own way.

I had literally no desire to sleep anymore. I sat in the living room, wide awake, all through the night. I'd just sit and stare, looking ahead, at nothing in particular. It was similar to going into a trance; I was physically there, but my mind was in a far off place.

I began to refer to these moments of deep thought as my "dark world". Some people like to meditate, and I'd describe it as being somewhat like that, except in my case it was nothing but darkness. If you've ever sat in a room in the middle of the night and been unable to see anything, then you probably have a general idea of what I'm talking about. Think about a place where there's no light and it's so dark, you can't even see your own hand.

That's the kind of place where I'd mentally go. There was literally nothing there. I enjoyed this state of mind because in my dark world there was no more pain, no more tears. There was nothing, and nothing was better in this particular case.

All through the night, I'd sit in my dark world and argue with God. Of course, there were literally hundreds of people who were already talking to God on our behalf through their prayers, and I'm sure they were asking God for things like keeping our family safe, giving us strength, and so forth.

However, my conversation with God was much different. I threw a lot of things at Him. "If You're so powerful, how could You allow this to happen? I thought You were a God of love? They say You gave Your son, so if You understand what that's like, how could You ever put me through this? Are You there? Do You even exist? I'd be a better God than You!"

I didn't hold back. I told Him exactly what I felt and thought. I made it clear I wasn't so sure He was anything close to what people thought He was, and I challenged Him over and over. I still couldn't sleep, and I just sat and argued throughout the night, but I never got any answers, never got a response, at least not for the first two nights.

On the third night, as I settled in for another

long night, my wife came and asked me an unusual question. She looked at me and inquired, "Has Seth come to you yet? Have you gotten your sign?" I found that to be really strange and unusual, because she'd never talked like that before; yet, here she was, grilling me as to whether or not I'd gotten a "sign."

When I sort of laughed and told her things didn't work that way, she never wavered. Her expression didn't change, and she firmly said she thought I would get my sign that very night.

Trish put one of Seth's toys on the fireplace mantel and said, "That may help."

She then abruptly decided it needed to be closer, so she moved the little figurine to the coffee table nearby. And with that, she went to the bedroom to lie down, once again leaving me alone to continue my nightly battle with God.

It was on this third night when my body finally gave out and I nodded off a little after two in the morning. My sleep didn't last long though, as around four o'clock I was jolted wide awake. I looked around in the darkness, expecting to see someone or something, but there was nothing to be seen; there was only silence. I sat there, wondering what had woken me when suddenly visions of Seth began flowing through my mind. It's hard to explain exactly what I was seeing, but it was sort of like reliving all the things Seth and I had shared. There were so many memories, and it felt so real, but one particular memory stood out from all the others.

Somehow, I knew I had to write down what I was seeing and feeling immediately; however, in the darkness of my mom's home, I couldn't see, and I had no idea where a pen or paper might be. Due to that situation, I did what people do these days and reached for my smart phone.

I should take a moment to explain that my sister, Angie, had set up a memorial page for Seth on Facebook, and she'd been updating people on what was going on using that site. Initially I didn't think much of the idea, but I did add the app to my phone so I could see the comments others were making. It also gave me the option to post something if I felt so inclined.

Sitting there in the dark that morning, with those visions floating in my head, I certainly felt the need to record everything; so, I grabbed my phone, logged on to the site, and wrote everything down. The words I wrote were heartfelt and expressive of where I was in that moment in time, and they went like this:

Every night Seth would ask me one question. Every single night it was the same question. It didn't matter if he was playing with his toys, watching TV or whatever else he may have been doing. Right around 9 pm he would ask me that question and he expected me to play his game.

The exchange would go like this: "Do you know what time it is?" Me: "Time for you to get a job?" Seth: "No." Me: "Time for you to clean your room?" Seth: "Noooo!" And we would continue back and forth until I responded with the correct "Is it Snuggle Time?" And Seth would give a resounding "YES". Then he would climb up on my lap, snuggle up against his daddy and stay that way until he fell asleep.

This happened every night. Snuggle Time was the highlight of my day and I believe it was Seth's as well. Snuggle Time in our home meant hugs, kisses, and unconditional love. Snuggle Time completed another day for us and allowed Seth to give and receive love, have a sense of security, and get the attention of his daddy to end his day.

Snuggle Time was pure. Snuggle Time was open and honest. Snuggle Time completed us. It didn't matter if I was reading, watching TV, browsing Facebook or anything else. When I heard "Do you know what time it is?" The world stopped so I could have Snuggle Time with my son.

I no longer will get to hear that question. Snuggle Time with Seth has come to an end, but at least I experienced it. Some people drink alcohol, do drugs, or find another way to experience a high. Snuggle Time replaced any need for that.

There was no better high than holding that child in my arms and receiving his little hugs and kisses and hear-

ing "I love you daddy" to finish my day. So now I ask all of you, "Do you know what time it is?" It's a game that we all need to play more often.

Maybe instead of play station, if the world replaced it with "Do you know what time it is" then this world would be a better place. Maybe children would grow up with less hate in their heart. Maybe there would be less violence. Maybe there would be more kindness. Maybe we all would feel more fulfilled.

Through all of this pain I at least can rest assured that Seth knew he was loved and I knew that I was loved in return. Both of us knew the answer before the question was asked. In our world it was always Snuggle Time.

Now ask yourself, "Do you know what time it is?

CHAPTER FIVE

The Cardinal Calls

L ater that morning, my wife made her way into the kitchen, where I sat staring out the window. She immediately asked me if I'd received my sign, and I responded with a simple no as I shook my head.

"I really thought you'd get it," she said with a sigh.

I quickly changed the subject and told her I wanted to go home. My wife gave me a stern look, letting me know she just wasn't ready to go yet. I completely understood why she felt that way, but I missed my dogs. I missed my bed. I missed my son. I wanted to be where we shared our moments, but for my wife, it was a different place now.

Trish had seen and dealt with things in our home I simply cannot imagine. She was traumatized in ways I don't know how I would handle. In fact, she's experienced Post Traumatic Stress Disorder, as a result of what she experienced, she still wakes up in the middle of the night with night terrors. I feel for her every day. She tries so hard to be strong for our daughter, but I see her struggles and feel her pain deeply.

On that particular morning, I just nodded my head and told her I understood. I then made the decision that I'd go to the house by myself. I'd pet the dogs. I'd take a shower in my bathroom. I'd get everyone a fresh change of clothes. I'd be home again, even if only for a few minutes.

Yet from the moment I walked in the front door of our house, I began to think I'd made a poor decision. I stood frozen in the doorway as I stared at the stained blue carpet where just a few days ago the paramedics had worked on my child.

My stomach churned, and I literally thought I was going to be sick. The tears welled up in my eyes, and I couldn't stop staring at that spot, reliving that moment all over again. The day of the accident, I'd been focused on tending to my wife, figuring out what was actually happening, and ensuring my son got the help he needed. There had been no time for me to worry about how I felt or to overthink the situation.

This time, it was much different. Now I was seeing the moment from an emotional standpoint, and believe it or not, it was much more difficult than the first time I'd experienced it. The raw emotions and tragic circumstances came crashing down on me, and I felt weaker than ever. I thought about walking back out and never coming back again.

Then Princess, our full-blooded German Shepherd, came running to greet me. She was excited, and her eagerness brought my mind back to the present moment; what a gift that was. I leaned over and petted her and spent a few moments treasuring the love a dog gives. I hadn't given it much thought, but this whole experience had to be traumatic for Princess as well.

When we brought Seth home from the hospital as a newborn, Princess immediately took to the baby. She would smell and gently nudge him with her nose. She would sit near him, wherever he was, in a protective, motherly mode.

Numerous times, she tried to take him from us while we held him; it was never a malicious thing, but rather an instinct she seemed to have to take the baby and care for it. We never bred Princess, so she never had puppies of her own, and I often wondered if, for her, Seth was her puppy.

Princess was there with Seth every step of the way, from his birth until his death. She slept in his room and let him roughhouse all over her. He would pull on her ears, tug on her tail, and pry open her mouth to look at her teeth, and she always obliged him. She loved him with all she was, and now suddenly he was gone. How difficult must that be for her? I hadn't even considered the trauma that our poor dog must have felt as everything unfolded.

After loving on Princess for a few minutes, I made my way to my bedroom and packed a fresh change of clothes for everyone. I then jumped into the shower, and as the warm water flowed, so did my tears. I didn't realize it at the time, but this would become a new ritual for me, one that involved taking my morning shower and sobbing like a small child as I allowed the pain of this new reality to overcome me. I'm not sure why, but the shower really seemed to bring out those feelings and the vulnerability that comes with them.

After my shower, I managed to compose myself, then emerged from the bedroom. I walked into the kitchen, and there stood my wife's sister, Linda. She and her husband had volunteered to stay at the house and help get things in order while we stayed at my mom's.

Linda looked at me and asked if I'd gotten my sign yet. I couldn't believe it. What was it that made these sisters think a person just magically got a sign after someone died? Had I married into some weird, cult-like family that believed in mystical and spiritual voodoo or something? It made no sense to me, as I firmly believed in science and scientific findings.

The concept of religion and spiritual things never came easy to me, so the idea that people got 'signs' wasn't something I ever seriously gave much thought to. It just didn't make sense in how I viewed the world; it's amazing how quickly things in life can change though.

I looked at Linda and told her I'd definitely not received a sign. She smiled and said, "I think you're about to," as she pointed out the kitchen window.

I shifted my attention out the window into our back yard, and what I saw took my breath away. The most beautiful red bird I'd ever gazed upon was sitting on a tree branch, staring directly into the house.

Cardinals are the state bird of Ohio, so seeing one isn't something anyone would necessarily call rare, but this one was different. He was easily the brightest red bird I'd ever seen. He literally glistened in the sun, and his eyes never seemed to wander from me. I was quickly drawn out the back door and towards that magnificent creature.

As soon as I opened the door to walk into the back yard, I could hear the cardinal chirping and singing up a storm. His sound was distinct, loud, and inviting. I felt like I needed to get a picture of him to show my wife, so I took out my phone, snapped a pic, and glanced at it. The picture didn't turn out the way I wanted, and I realized I'd need to get closer if I wanted a really good one.

So, I slowly made my way towards the bird as he continued chirping. I got within several feet of him and was ready to take my second picture when he grew silent. I was worried I'd scared him and he was going to fly off, so I stood there silently. However, the beautiful bird didn't fly away; instead, he simply began to jump from branch to branch and slowly move along the tree line.

He would jump a few branches, stop, look back at me, and chirp. Instinctively, I began to follow him. When he stopped, I stopped. When he moved, I moved. We continued this dance every few feet, and during each stop, the bird would look at me and chirp before moving on.

Eventually, the cardinal stopped completely and began to chirp loudly and more frenzied than before. I wasn't sure why he was suddenly so worked up, but I decided to change the game myself by emulating him. Each time I began to do my best cardinal impression, he would grow silent, listen to me, then as soon as I stopped, he would start back up again. It was a surreal moment to say the least. This interaction between the two of us was simply amazing for me in that moment.

Our back-and-forth conversation went on for what seemed like several minutes, then a voice in my head told me to look down. Now, I don't mean a literal voice of course, but it was clear and distinct. Something told me to look down, so I did.

Lying there directly between my feet was a baseball. And I don't mean there was a baseball near me or in my general vicinity, rather it was literally between both my feet, in a direct line between the toes of my shoes.

This particular baseball was especially meaningful. It was the ball Seth had lost the weekend before his death. The kids had been out in the back yard playing, and the ball had been lost; now, it was found.

My daughter later explained Seth had been worried I'd be upset they'd lost it, which sounded a lot like Seth. He always wanted others to be happy and proud of him, so the idea that he lost one of his dad's baseballs would have bothered him quite a lot.

So now here I was, leaning over and picking up what had been a lost-ball. I smiled as I looked at the cardinal again. "Is this my sign?" I asked him. He began to chirp again frantically and loudly, then suddenly he flew away.

Could this actually have been my sign? Did things really work that way? Was it all merely a coincidence? You can certainly argue that I wanted a better picture, so I followed the bird down the tree line and he was merely trying to get away from me. You could say I just happened to stumble across the ball. I think that would be a perfectly logical and fair way of looking at it and I wouldn't blame you if you did.

However, if you believe God does listen to us and loves us, then I think it's also fair to say I likely did receive a sign that day. In that moment, when I was at my weakest, when I needed something to keep me going, that little red bird gave me a sign. More importantly, he gave me hope.

I couldn't wait to get back to my mom's house to share my story with my wife and anyone else who would listen. For the first time since that tragic day, I felt like maybe, just maybe things would get better. I truly believed my cardinal encounter was a difference maker, but I had no idea just how important that bird would become in our lives going forward.

I went back to my mother's home and excitedly shared the story about my interaction with the bird to everyone I talked to that day. There was something about it that had inspired me to keep going.

I felt a bit stronger, and I suddenly felt like I needed to speak at Seth's funeral. I hadn't planned to do that up to that point, but now I had a message to deliver, one of love and hope. People needed to hear it. I needed to share it. The only question was whether or not I could find the strength to stand up at my son's funeral and deliver an actual speech.

Could I maintain my composure long enough to

deliver the message? It seemed like I was asking myself to perform an awfully big task, but it was something I knew I needed to try. Something inside me was telling me it wasn't a choice.

CHAPTER SIX

Minute By Minute

After making my decision to speak at the funeral, I revisited Seth's memorial page on Facebook and began reading all the comments. It warmed my heart seeing how many people were expressing their condolences, love, and support for our family.

My initial disdain for the site quickly changed, and soon I found myself sharing my own thoughts and feelings on it on a regular basis. After I requested that people share their memories of Seth, the site quickly filled with amazing tributes and stories.

This was going to be more than a speech; it was going to be an amazing tribute. However, I knew there was a good chance I may still not be able to deliver the entire speech and needed someone as my backup; that way, if I did break down, the speech would still be delivered.

So, I picked up the phone and called Troy. I asked if he'd be my backup, and I'd barely finished asking before he was saying yes. He told me he'd be honored to be a part of Seth's final day, so we spent several hours that evening coming up with just the right presentation. It had to be absolutely perfect, and by the time we were done, it was.

I like to believe we were guided by a higher power when we created the program, because it all came together better than I ever could have imagined.

With that out of the way, there was still another hurdle to be faced. Before the funeral itself, we had to endure the showing, and that would be no small task in itself.

Our small town, Cardington, is located about forty miles north of Columbus. It's one of those small, one-stoplight country towns where the farmers are appreciated and where knows your name. It's the kind of place where, as a kid, you cannot wait to leave, and it's the kind of place where, as an adult, you want to live and raise your kids.

As we drove through the downtown area the day of the showing, something seemed different. The entire town just had this sad feel to it. It was incredibly eerie, and that eerie feeling got even more intense as we pulled into the funeral home.

I looked across the street at the youth baseball fields and let out a heavy sigh. Life and death so close to one another. On one side of the street was a place full of fun, games, cheers, and fond memories. On the other side of the street...well, it was altogether something else.

Even more ironic was the fact that I'd actually scheduled this very day to be the first day of ball practice. We could just as easily have been on the other side of the road that day; yet, we weren't.

Seth had been super-excited to start his first year of baseball...well, I called it baseball, but he always corrected me and told me it wasn't baseball; it was t-ball. He had adamantely informed me it was not real baseball, because you don't pitch. He had a valid point, so I tried to remember to call it t-ball whenever the subject came up.

After years of coaching at the upper levels, I had been really excited about dropping down to coach my son. Seth was ready to go, too. He had lived in the gym and on the ball fields since birth and had already developed all the skills he needed to be successful.

In fact, the previous year I had helped coach my daughter in Little League Baseball, so Seth was always there at practices, hitting off the tees, and playing catch. After games, he would demand I pitch him an entire bucket of balls so he could hit and run the bases.

Seth would put on that helmet, the one that was way too big for his little head, then trudge out to home plate, dragging his bat behind him, leaving a line in the sand; however, when he got into his stance at the plate, it was all business. His face showed complete focus, his eyes locked on the ball, and his swing was pretty darn good for a five-year-old.

He would drive the ball up the middle of the field, then take off running. Of course, he would sprint around the bases and slide into home with a big grin, enjoying his victory. As much as I loved coaching my daughter in those two-hour games, I enjoyed the ten-minute post-game sessions with my son every bit as much.

My mind jolted back to where we were and the task at hand. It was time to go into the funeral home, and we slowly made our way to the front door. I was going to see my son in his t-ball uniform for the first time. My wife had decided Seth would wear the uniform he never got to wear in life but had been eagerly waiting for the entire year. I agreed with that decision wholeheartedly.

I cannot put into words what it was like walking into the funeral home that day. I've spent a lot of time stuck right here while writing this book. I wanted to explain it, to put it in a way that made sense, but I can't. There are no words to describe what it was like walking in there, no words that can put my emotions in the right context, so I'll just leave it at that, and we'll just move on with the story.

The showing started at 2:00 PM and did not stop until well after 8:00 PM. We were supposed to have a two-hour break to rest, but there was a constant line the entire time, so that break never came. I was told it took over an hour to get in; yet, despite the long line, people waited, viewed, and expressed their condolences.

As difficult as the day was, it reminded me yet again how lucky we were to live in a small town where people care about one another. It also reminded me how many lives Seth touched in his short time here. The funeral director later told me he thought the entire town turned out.

He may have been right, but the only thing I knew for sure was that I was emotionally drained. I wasn't sure how I was going to make it through the next day, but we'd developed the mantra, "One hour, one minute, one second at a time." That's what it takes in moments like these.

CHAPTER SEVEN

Let's Do This

The day of the funeral came, and I found myself feeling really nervous. I wasn't sure if I was scared, upset, or merely anxious about trying to deliver Seth's message to the people attending.

I couldn't decide what to wear either. I kept going back and forth between dress shirts and pants, and nothing seemed right. I then found myself thinking, *What would Seth want me to wear?* It wouldn't be some old stuffy dress clothes. That much I was certain of.

What exactly would Seth pick out if he got to choose? That question was actually easy enough for me to answer, so I pulled out my Ohio State football jersey. You see, every Saturday during college football season, Seth and I would spend our time in front of the television, wearing our OSU jerseys and rooting for the Buckeyes. He called that our "boy time" and would always say there were "no girl" allowed.

Seth even had a set of mini-football helmets that included every Big Ten team, and on Saturdays during the season he'd pull them out and match up the teams that were playing. He could name every college by their helmet, and he'd spend his time carefully putting them all in their proper places for the day.

Seth enjoyed the whole college football experience, and this had been the year I was going to take him to his very first Ohio State game at the Horseshoe; so, deciding what to wear became very clear at that moment in time. We needed one last "boy day." I just hoped he wouldn't be mad at me, because this time the girls were going to be there, too.

The service was held at a local church, and once there, I started having difficulty dealing with the emotions. I snuck away and went into the downstairs restroom. Of course, it wasn't long before people came looking for me. I was just feeling overwhelmed, and the tears were already overcoming me. There was no way I could deliver a speech in front of everyone. I just couldn't do it.

Right as I was resigned to giving up, Joel Partlow walked into the restroom and said, quite possibly, the only thing that could have been said to me at that moment. His words will forever be with me, and it changed my frame of mind as soon as he said them. What were his words? He simply said, "Fourth quarter, Coach. Let's do this." Just like that, I somehow felt stronger.

Joel, along with myself and another parent named Chuck Jones, had coached our girls in youth basketball for several years, so the three of us knew each other well. All of the time spent in the gym together also meant that basketball was another thing that Seth was exposed to on a regular basis.

In our most recent season, Seth had become more involved as my "assistant coach." He would imitate me as I coached, pacing along the sideline. He had his own whistle and would literally tell the girls what they were doing wrong whenever he noticed something.

One day, we were playing a game, and the girls were having a bad day. A really bad day. They weren't running their offense, their defense was lazy, and as the coach, I was getting very frustrated, mainly because we were actually a really good team and seeing their lack of effort wasn't acceptable. So, I called a time out and chastised the kids. As I did, Seth was right there in the huddle, holding his dry erase board and listening intently.

After the time out, the girls trotted back out on

the floor, and that's when Seth tugged on my shirt. I looked down, and he showed me the board he was holding. He'd scribbled a bunch of lines and a few circles on it, and he looked at me and said, "I drew a play so the girls can play better."

In my irritated state, I sarcastically said to my son, "Well, that looks exactly like what we're running." However, Seth didn't get the sarcasm, and instead he puffed out his little chest and smiled as he proudly took his seat on the bench.

Here was my child, with a pure heart, participating and trying to help, and I initially passed it off as meaningless. Luckily for me, he heard me say, "Great job. I appreciate it." Isn't it funny how sometimes it's the little kids who have to remind us of what's important in life? I know I learned a valuable lesson that day.

So now it was the fourth quarter, a time when you may be tired, worn down. You may feel drained, and you may think you aren't able to go on - but if you're a true competitor, then you love the fourth quarter.

It's that time for one final push, a point in time where you have to rise up. You have to be willing to dig down deep inside and give everything you have left.

The fourth quarter separates the good teams from the bad ones, and it separates the great teams from the good ones. The fourth quarter can be the difference between winning and losing. That's what the fourth quarter means, and Joel's coach speak was just what I needed.

I composed myself, looked in the mirror, and told myself, "Fourth quarter. Let's do this."

When I was finally called up to the podium, I realized just how packed the church was. There was literally no room left in the place, and I looked out at many familiar faces. As I stood there, I suddenly felt weak, and once again the doubt crept in. I wasn't sure how this was going to play out.

I introduced two young guest speakers, Michael Parker and Alyson Moore, and let them read speeches they had prepared. Michael made it through his speech, precise and to the point. Meanwhile, Alyson struggled with her emotions, and I understood. I moved to her side to let her know I was right there with her. She choked back the tears, then she, too, did a wonderful job, delivering her message of love.

Troy then took the stage to read many of the beautiful messages others had written about Seth. As I listened to the things he was reading, I realized there was a recurring theme. Everything was about Seth's infectious smile, how he lit up a room when he came in, his big hugs, and how he made others feel special. It, too, was about his love.

When it was my turn to speak, I eased into it

by talking about how the Snuggle Time story had already reached almost 200,000 people and was being shared not only in the United States, but around the world. It had reached Japan, Germany, Ireland, England, Australia, Canada, and a few other countries.

We were receiving messages from people all over the place who wanted us to know Seth's message was making a difference in their lives. The Snuggle Time message was impactful, meaningful, and people were responding to it.

At that point, I got weak yet again. The tears welled up, and as I stumbled backwards, I felt Troy standing there behind me, ready to step in. My hands were shaking, and I got quiet.

The entire church was silent, as everyone just watched intently to see what I would say or do next. A voice inside my head then asked me a question and it did so with a force that I could not ignore: Are you to going to be a typical grieving parent who lost a child, or are you going to suck it up and deliver the message? A bit harsh, I suppose, but that's what I heard.

Now, no one would have blamed me if I sat down and acted like a grieving parent; I *was* a grieving parent. However, it was still the fourth quarter, and I wasn't done yet. I couldn't be. So, I stepped back up to the microphone with more determination than before.

My voice rose as I spoke and I delivered Seth's Snuggle Time message with a power I didn't even know I had. Everyone's eyes were focused on me as I spoke about love, moments that matter, and my son's final message to us all.

After about fifteen minutes of preaching, I sat down. I'm not sure if there was a dry eye in the house. I could tell people felt my emotion, my pain. As for me, I felt a sense of relief. My job was done. The message had been delivered, and now I could go back to being that grieving parent. The fourth quarter was over, and we were victorious.

After the service, we were waiting outside to begin our short drive to the cemetery. As the procession pulled out of the church parking lot, a light snow began to fall. As we passed through downtown, the snow continued, but as we turned into the cemetery, it suddenly stopped.

At the grave site, the sky remained cloudy and gray, and the wind sent a cold chill through all of us, yet ater the graveside service ended, the skies cleared, the sun came out, and the wind died down. The weather seemed to be in perfect sync with the service, and others noticed.

The funeral reception was held at the local American Legion Hall, as we had anticipated a large crowd. By the time we walked in, the room was already filled, and it seemed like everyone wanted to talk to us about the weather. It appeared others were beginning to watch and look for signs, too. In that moment, I began to realize everyone was just like me. They were all looking for hope, because none of us had the answers.

During the reception several people talked to me about how they were impressed by my speech and with the Snuggle Time story. Others wanted to tell me how strong I was, and several said they could never do what I did.

The truth is, I didn't view myself as impressive in any way, and I certainly was not strong. I just did what I had to do for my son: I delivered his message. Wouldn't any parent do anything they can for their child? That's how I viewed it. I delivered Seth's Snuggle Time message because he couldn't. I was his voice.

The true beauty of the message connecting with others came from my cousin's husband, Shane. Shane told me that, as a father, the Snuggle Time message moved him in a deeply profound way. As he sat in the church earlier and listened to the words I shared, he thought about his own relationships with his kids.

He had tears in his eyes as he told me he felt he could do a better job as a father and my story had made him want to do exactly that. Those were just the words I wanted to hear. Those were just the words I *needed* to hear. To know Seth's death could mean something and his message was being received in the way it was meant to be was all I could have hoped for.

Throughout the reception, people repeatedly wished us well, but more importantly, I kept hearing how Seth's Snuggle Time message was resounding in ways I never expected. People were deeply moved and emotional. I knew then something really special would come from it, but I still didn't realize the full impact it would eventually have.

CHAPTER EIGHT

The Florida-Georgia Line

As difficult as the days had been so far, I knew the days ahead would be even tougher. Eventually, people would go back to their own lives, and we would be left alone to pick up the pieces. Worse yet was the fact that I wasn't sure how I was going to get my wife to move back into our home.

After everything she'd experienced, I couldn't blame her for wanting to be anywhere but there. The fact that our child had died in our home was just another horrible layer in a tragic situation. How were we going to be able to accept that fact?

With that in mind, I reached out to Troy yet again. I met him at the house and we walked through it room by room, discussing the changes I thought may be good: Tearing out the stained carpet, painting the walls, and maybe getting some new furniture.

My thought was that if we could change up the feel of the place, maybe, just maybe we could somehow start anew. Nothing was ever going to be the same, so why not give the entire house a facelift?

Troy was intent and purposeful, writing things down as we discussed them. We made a must-do list, then a wish-list. The idea was to be sure we did the things we felt were most important, which was enough for me.

However, Troy also pushed to include the things I'd like to see, if it was possible. So, we made both lists, and I gave him a budget I thought we could handle. He told me one way or another, he'd be sure we had a new home to come back to in just a few days.

Feeling confident that Troy would be able to get the work done, I turned my attention back to trying to figure out how to heal my family. Fixing a house was one thing, but fixing myself was going to be quite another. I wasn't sure how I was going to do that, let alone how I was going to help everyone else, but that seemed like my next task.

I had an aunt, Linda Mathews, who knew the pain we were enduring all too well. Linda had lost her own son, Tony, many years before this moment, so she'd already been there. Linda and Uncle Ron had both suffered in the same way Trish and I now were; so, we spent a lot of time talking about how they handled it and tried to heal.

I never realized how difficult it was when my cousin Tony died. For me it was easy enough. I went to the showing, to the funeral, to the family functions. I was there, but I failed to fathom what they were all going through. Now that I do know I wish that I didn't and I regret not understanding their pain originally.

Linda shared with me that she and her daughters, Stacey and Nikki, had gone to counseling, but Ron never did. I didn't find that surprising, because most dads tend to handle things much differently than moms do. While females typically feel the need to talk about it, males will probably bury themselves in their work, finding some way to keep busy so they don't have to think about the problem. Some people say this is a poor way to handle it, but that's the way it seems to be.

As for me, I was finding that writing my thoughts down and putting my pain, emotions, and feelings into words was therapeutic. That was my counseling. I'd later find out many therapists actually recommend doing exactly that as a way to cope. I did not know that when I did it, but I did know it felt good to express myself through written words.

Linda had quietly spearheaded a movement that saw several family members pitch in to send us to Florida for a week. She explained to me that after their son died, getting away for a little while to clear their heads had helped them as a family, so she wanted to be sure we had the chance to do the same. Thankfully, we have some amazing family members, and they did not hesitate to help make that trip a reality.

I felt even more thankful when I learned Uncle Harold and Sue Copeland, our family in Florida, agreed to have us spend that time with them in Sarasota. We hadn't seen them in several years, so the idea of the trip just kept getting better, and I soon found myself eager to go. If you haven't noticed yet, I come from a rather large family, and that's an amazing thing in times of need, to say the least. The power of family is truly like no other.

When the day finally came, I loaded the suitcases while my wife, daughter, mom, and yet another aunt, Barb Copeland, all piled into the van. Soon enough, we were heading down Interstate 75 for the long trek to Florida. We ended up driving straight through, and if you've ever driven south down Interstate 75, you know it seems to take an eternity to get through the state of Georgia.

There is nothing wrong with the Peach State, but once you get through Atlanta, you feel like you've accomplished a major milestone in life. I say that for two main reasons. First, when driving from Ohio to Florida it seems as if Atlanta is that last big hurdle on your way to the sunshine and beaches. Secondly, you simply do not want to hit rush hour in Atlanta. One year we did exactly that, and the rush hour coupled with ongoing highway repairs caused us to spend several hours sitting in traffic. On this particular trip, we hit Atlanta at two in the morning, so it was basically traffic-free, and we sailed along on the seventeen-hour drive to our destination.

As we finally were nearing the Florida-Georgia line, an older dance song called "99 Red Balloons" came on the radio. I looked over at my wife, and she looked back at me. Trish smiled, and I knew what she was thinking. This was one of Seth's favorite 80s songs.

Of course, his favorite color was also red. I recalled how he said this particular song made him "want to dance" and he would always wiggle and move around when he heard it.

Trish and I talked about how that was the perfect song to hear as we prepared to enter the State of Florida that early morning. Seth wasn't with us on the trip, but at that time it felt like he was. There was a feeling of happiness and sadness combined in that moment, and then, right as we crossed the border, the song ended, and in its place a Kenny Loggins song came on. The words "I'm alright, nobody worry about me" blared out of the radio. Once again, Trish and I looked at each other and just smiled.

We get it, little buddy. We get it. You're with us. Welcome to Florida.

CHAPTER NINE

Beauty All Around Us

Trish was feeling sick and not up to doing anything that first day at my uncle's home, and nobody could blame her. We'd been through so much, and the stress was difficult to manage. So, she decided to stay and rest while the rest of us took a trip to a pier Uncle Harold thought we'd enjoy.

It turned out he was right, very right. As we parked, I immediately noticed how beautiful the beach and water both looked. It was a sunny day, and the sand glistened. As we began our walk along the path towards the pier, I noticed how gorgeous the palm trees were as they hung over our walkway.

I grabbed my phone and beckoned the family so I could get a few pictures. As I snapped the pics, I noticed the big rocks just off the beach area. That looked like the ideal spot for another picture, so I asked my daughter to walk out there and pose. Of course, I got the teenager eye-roll and a little complaining, but eventually she did, and I managed to get a few gorgeous pictures of her. Everything was just about perfect at that moment in time, at least as perfect as it could be.

After getting a few more pictures, we proceeded out onto the long pier towards a restaurant that had been built on the far end. People were fishing, and birds were soaring all around us. The old boards creaked with every step we took, and there were no rails, so you felt like you just might fall in - but even that didn't seem to be that bad of an option at that moment in time.

As we reached the end of the pier, I stopped and just gazed in wonderment. The view was magnificent. The water stretched for miles. There were no boats or any kind of activity on the water at all. I could make out a bridge that spanned across the water far away. It was a breathtaking view, and it made me feel so alive. It was something I truly needed; it was as if God Himself knew it and said, "Take a look at this my child."

My attention was diverted when I heard someone call out, "Dolphin."

My head snapped to my left, because I certainly didn't want to miss this! At first I didn't see him, but then he came into view and neared us. We spent the next twenty minutes watching in amazement as the dolphin frolicked and played like a little child about 30 yards away.

Eventually, the dolphin made his way away from the pier, towards the beach. It was at that moment when I realized that there wasn't just one dolphin, but many of them. I counted at least four and they all seemed to be enjoying showing off for everyone. It was truly a sight to behold.

After enjoying the amazing school of dolphins for several more minutes, we finally made our way back up the pier and towards the shore. As we walked along, I looked in the water and noticed a baby-sized stingray swim into view. That was pretty cool in itself, but then it jumped out of the water, flipped directly beside us, and landed with a splash back into the water. It continued to swim along with us and jumped out of the water a second time, then yet a third before finally disappearing back into the deeper waters of the ocean.

Aunt Sue commented that she had heard of that kind of thing happening before, but in all her years living in Florida, she had never actually seen one do it. She laughed and said it was "just a little kid showing off for us." It was definitely a little kid, and it sure seemed like it was showing off for us. Just like the dolphins.

Once we reached the shore, Harold and I wandered away from the others and out onto the beach. As we stood and looked out over the ocean once again, he shared some profound words with me. I cannot quote them now, but basically he told me how in life we never know what we're going to get. Some days, everything goes our way; other days, nothing is going to work. It's never going to make complete sense, but we have to keep going forward, because we can't go back.

Harold may not have realized it, but the words he shared with me that day helped shape me. In that perfect moment, with the gorgeous surroundings, beautiful ocean view, frolicking dolphins, baby stingray, and then his encouraging words, I was shown how my life was *not* actually over. I was reminded there was still more to see.

I will never forget that day. The pure beauty I witnessed. Of course, nothing would change the fact that Seth was gone. Nothing ever will. But it did remind me of the amazing beauty the world still holds. It allowed me to see things I'd never seen before, things I'd forgotten all about.

Life is like that. There's beauty all around us, but we sometimes live in a funnel and fail to notice it. Going forward, I hope my eyes stay open. I guess only time will tell.

CHAPTER TEN

Disney in a Day

W e'd originally promised to take our daughter to Disney World for a day while in Florida, but now that the time was near, we were not sure we could do it. Could we spend an entire day watching all those parents with their children? All those little kids smiling, laughing, and creating new memories... memories we could never have.

It seemed like a tall task, and it just did not feel like the right place for us to be at that point in time. When we told our daughter we were thinking we'd skip the Disney trip, she agreed, but her face showed her disappointment.

Alex had been looking forward to going there for a long time. She and Seth both. In fact, Seth had one of those big crayon banks. If you remember them, you know they look like a giant crayon, sit on the floor, and come up about waist high. Well, Seth had been putting all his change into that giant yellow crayon bank more than a year. He would beg for our change so he could add it to his "Disney" money.

As we thought about Seth saving his money and the look of disappointment that crept onto our daughters' face when we said we were not going, we reversed our decision and decided we would indeed go to Disney for a day.

On that Easter Sunday, we loaded up early in the morning and began the two-hour drive from Sarasota over to Orlando. Normally, I don't think we would have even considered going to a theme park on a day like Easter, but at that moment we weren't really thinking about holidays. We weren't thinking about going to church or spending time with family. We were in a haze, just somehow trying to get through each day. So although it was Easter, it did not register in our minds as anything more than just another day on the calendar.

We arrived just prior to the park opening, and as we stood in line to buy our tickets, I looked around at the parents with small children, then glanced over at my wife. I could see the hurt in her eyes, but she seemed to be holding up alright so far.

I purchased three of what they call the "Park Hopper" ticket. With that kind of admission you can go from park-to-park as you desire all day long for one price. That seemed like our best bet; if things got too uncomfortable in the Magic Kingdom Park, we could simply leave and go to Epcot or MGM Studios. Of course I anticipated the Magic Kingdom would be the park that might have most of the younger kids, considering its home to Mickey Mouse, so we would go there first and see how things went.

I honestly had no idea what to expect and just decided we would deal with things as they came. What else can you do in a situation like that?

After securing our tickets, I knew we would need to board the monorail to be transported to the actual park. I remembered that from our trip there when Alex was just a little one herself. What I did not remember was people losing their minds when the gates opened! All of a sudden, people began jumping lines and cutting one another off with their selfish need to be the very first to board the monorail.

It quickly became a dangerous and frightening scene, as people around us showed absolutely no regard for the safety or well-being of others. One small child actually fell as her mother dragged her by the arm in a mad rush to get up the ramp. The mother never missed a beat though; she just scooped up her now crying toddler and ran as fast as she could.

We were appalled by the behavior. Maybe it was because of what we had just gone through, but what we witnessed that day was disturbing to say the least, and I hope Disney has since learned to manage the opening a bit better than that. If they have not, I highly recommend you think twice about trying to go right at the start of the day. Now, the Disney experience is like no other, and I am certainly not saying to avoid going. In fact it has always been one of our favorite places, but on that day the negative side of human behavior created a poor experience for us...well, at least a poor start to the day.

Once we boarded the monorail, things got a bit better, and after we made our way into Magic Kingdom, the crowd was very manageable. I let out a deep sigh as I stood at the entrance, looking towards Cinderella's Castle.

We made it, Seth, went through my mind. *We made it.*

After a quick review of one of the Magic Kingdom maps we decided to make our way to one of our favorite rides first: The Pirates of the Caribbean. As we approached the attraction, we were shocked to see there was no line! That was a pleasant surprise, to say the least.

We walked up, loaded onto the small boat, and were immediately whisked away into a world of fantasy. It was great to sit there on that ride that morning. Everything from the smells to the action of the pirates to the music, and just the entire ambiance allowed us to escape the reality and sorrow we were living, even for just a few minutes. The ride ended entirely too quickly, but it was an amazing way to start things off.

Later, as we stood in line for another ride, Trish was handed a red tag. The tag was Disney's way of measuring how long it took for a person to get from the entry to the actual ride, so they would randomly give them out to people. In our case, the fact that it was Seth's favorite color meant something extra special to my wife, and the fact that she was the one to receive it made her smile.

That in itself was good to see. Even more interesting to me though was that she received those red tags several times that morning, including three times in a row. The rest of us never received one; just her. I firmly believe we all get these little signs in our lives, and I know at that moment she needed it the most. So, she got it.

As I mentioned previously, we had purchased what they call the "Park Hopper" tickets and this meant we could move around from park to park throughout the day, so we did just that. We rode all the major rides we wanted to in the Magic Kingdom, then we headed over to Epcot.

There we visited several attractions, and while waiting in one line, we witnessed a parent yelling at their child. The young boy was probably three or four years old, and he was obviously very tired. He was acting out like young, tired kids do, and the parents were frustrated. The father was not calmly correcting his son's behavior; instead, he was telling him to quit being "a little brat" and to "knock it off" before he got spanked. My wife and I cringed. It was all we could do to bite our tongues in that moment.

Now, do not misunderstand me, as the entire situation was totally understandable. The parents were probably hot and tired themselves. The park was now crowded, and their child was a bit out of control - but for us, in that moment, when our minds wanted nothing more than to hold our child again, watching this interaction was extremely painful.

We could not understand how they did not just appreciate the fact that they had this incredible opportunity to create such positive memories. They had the one thing we wanted more than anything in the world. It was something we could not have, and we gladly would have taken Seth acting out and embarrassing us in that line that day. In fact, nothing would have made that day better; if he were only here.

If we had not experienced the traumatic event of losing our son, we would not have seen that situation the way we did. We would not have grasped how important every second, of each minute, of every day is. Of course, we never said a word to those parents, but I hope they at least enjoyed their day overall.

When we finally made it to MGM Studios, we had an interaction that was a bit awkward, to say the least. A young man working the ticket entry area looked at me and said, "I'm sorry for your loss."

I stopped in my tracks. *What? How did he know? How could this young man in Florida possibly know who we were or that we had lost our son?*

I was completely dumbfounded and shocked by his comment, and he must have seen my facial expression, because he pointed to my shirt and asked if I was a Buckeye fan. It was then I realized I was wearing one of my Ohio State shirts. The Buckeyes basketball team had recently lost in the NCAA basketball tournament, so this was the reference the young man was making.

My eyes filled with tears, and I let out a deep sigh of relief. "We just lost our five-year-old son, and I thought you were talking about that," I said to him, trying to explain my weird reaction to his comment.

I did not even consider that telling him we had just lost our child would make him feel bad. The poor kid had a look of horror on his face and said how sorry he was. He then asked us to wait to the side of the line.

He disappeared for a few minutes, and when he reappeared, he had a handful of "Fast Pass" tickets for us to use. These passes would get us through the park lines faster and certainly make our time there more enjoyable. It was his way of expressing his condolences for us in that moment. He then told us again how sorry he was for our loss, and we thanked him for the kind gesture. It was a heartfelt moment, and our family will always remember that young man for his actions.

Believe it or not, we made it through every park and rode every major ride all in one day. Those Fast Pass tickets helped of course! I have since joked we must have set some kind of Disney record, because there is no way you can make it through every park and ride everything you want all in a single day. That just does not happen. Yet it did. All the parks were extremely busy as the day wore on, but somehow it did not slow us down. That in itself was amazing.

My daughter enjoyed the day immensely, so I was glad we had chosen to attend. As for me and Trish, we struggled a lot. We just were not ready. At times I felt like we had wasted our money, because we truly could not enjoy the "Happiest Place on Earth." But then I think about the numerous smiles my daughter had and how we accomplished something she seemed to want so badly.

When I think of it now, I actually believe it was

Allie's way of honoring her brother. It was the trip we had planned but never took. It was the one Seth had saved for, so his sister wanted to complete it - for him. When I think of it that way, I am ok with spending those dollars. Who knows, maybe one day we will have the chance to go back for another family trip. Maybe one day Disney World will make us smile again.

CHAPTER ELEVEN

I See Jesus in Your Tree

By the end of our week in Florida, we were ready to go home. It was time to get back and figure out how we were going to live the rest of our lives. It was going to be a huge adjustment, and I knew we were in for a difficult road. That week away had given me a different perspective, but it did not change the fact that we had to learn to live again. How could we do it without Seth? That was the million dollar question and I was not sure how to answer it yet.

As we headed out onto the highway, all I could think about was Seth. My mind was focused yet again on the pain, and we drove along in silence. By the time we passed through Atlanta, I was ready to let my wife take a turn driving for a little while. I wanted the chance to look at Seth's Facebook page and read the posts that had accumulated. I also wanted to look at pictures of him.

I needed to see him again. I was hurting so much, and it seemed to be getting worse as we drove north.

As I scrolled through the pictures on my phone, I decided I would go ahead and post another picture of Seth. So, I chose a picture from his last Christmas. He was sitting on the floor next to the Christmas tree, opening a present. It was adorable, and it tore my heart open, but it felt like the right one to share. So, I did. Or at least I thought I did.

I had literally just posted the picture when I got a message from a friend of the family. The message said, "I see Jesus in your picture! His face is right there in the middle of the tree!" was the message.

Now, I don't know about you, but that was not a comment I was expecting. Jesus in my Christmas tree? More messages rolled in with people saying they were seeing it, too.

The entire idea seemed really farfetched to me, so I went back onto Facebook to take a look. What I found astounded me, but not for the reason you might think. What shocked me was that the picture I had carefully chosen was not the one that had posted. What people were seeing was the picture I had taken of my cardinal encounter. Now, I had no intention of ever sharing that, because it was a rather poor picture. You could not even make the bird out very well; yet, there it was.

I left Facebook, went back to the picture list on

my phone, and scrolled down through the pics. I was confused as to how that could have happened. I assumed the two pictures were near each other and I must have accidentally hit the wrong one; however, the pictures were nowhere near close, so there was no way I would have "accidentally" posted the wrong picture. I could not explain how the cardinal picture posted. There was no logical reason. It should not have happened; yet, it did.

I went back onto Facebook and looked at the picture again. I still thought it was a very poor picture, and I certainly did not see any faces. It just looked like a bad pic to me, which was why I never shared it before. Yet people were still sending me private messages and commenting. They could not believe what they were seeing. They were calling it a blessing. As for me, I still didn't see anything.

Eventually, after zooming in on the pic and analyzing it over and over, I finally realized what they were talking about. It became clear as could be. Right in the middle of the picture above the cardinal, there did appear to be a face. I could not argue with their interpretation that it looked like Jesus, because it did have that feel to it. Once I saw it, I was surprised at how I could have missed it. It was right there. Now, others who have looked at the picture have said they do not see anything, and I cannot argue with them, because it took me a while to see it myself, but once I did, it certainly made me think.

I was at another low point in my life, and somehow, right when I needed it, the cardinal came back into play. People were seeing something in that picture, and maybe on its own I could discard it simply as wishful thinking, but it was more than that for me. After my original interaction with the bird, I had a sense something more powerful than what I could explain had occurred. I talked about getting my "sign" and how the cardinal had acted in such an unusual manner. So, would it be unreasonable to think a higher power was somehow involved in that experience?

This is the part of my story I have not discussed much with others. My reasoning is simple. If I talk about it, then, inevitably, people want to see the picture. That then leads to a discussion about whether or not they see a face, which becomes the focal point – do you or don't you see it? It becomes all about something I do not really consider all that important.

I just don't think it matters if others see a face or not. What I focus on is the fact that the picture never should have posted to begin with! But it did, and then others made comments that caused me to look at and re-evaluate my life yet again. What I thought I already knew about the way things worked was constantly being challenged.

In that instance, I really felt like I was being

spoken to just when I needed it the most. What matters to me is that yet again the cardinal lifted me up when I needed something in my life to give me another boost of hope. I was once again reminded I don't have all the answers and just need to trust.

That is not so easy to do, but it sure seemed like the cardinal was going to continue to remind me of that fact. That is the message I want to discuss when I talk about the picture, but others want to debate whether or not the face of Jesus is there. I get it.

The idea of a face being in the picture is much more entertaining, so I will let you in on a little secret. There is more than one face (or so they say). Some say they see a little boy with a backwards hat on just below the Jesus face (some say he's sitting on his lap). Some say there is a warrior angel in the upper left corner of the picture, watching, maybe protecting everything.

Personally, I'm curious what the weird outline around the cardinal is. It looks to me a lot like the Star Wars robot R2D2. I don't know. If you want to analyze the picture, just go to whenthecardinalcalls.com, and you will find it there. Maybe you will see something, maybe you won't, but it's posted for anyone who finds the concept interesting.

What really made me stop and think though was the fact that I had fully intended to delete that picture. It was never meant to be seen, yet somehow it ended up being seen by many. And regardless of whether you think the face of Jesus is in that picture or not, the mere fact that others immediately reached out to me and made such a claim is mind-blowing.

After my original interaction with the cardinal, I felt the experience was something much greater than I could explain, and now others were confirming what I'd felt that day, that something bigger was probably at work. I felt like it was God's way of once again reminding me I was not as smart as I thought. The cardinal once again brought me peace just when I needed it the most. After that, the rest of the drive back to Ohio was a little easier to make, and that in itself was a relief.

CHAPTER TWELVE

Returning Home

U pon returning to Ohio, we were ready to go home, but Troy and I had earlier decided we would not go to our house until the morning after our return from Florida. We would spend the night at my mother's home one final time, which would allow everyone who had worked on our home to be there when we returned the next day.

While we were away, a lot of people in our community had signed up to help remodel our house. There were family members, friends, neighbors, and general acquaintances from the community who just cared. There were people who were good with tools, people who could paint, people who were good at landscaping, and people who did the running around and provided food to everyone helping.

Each and every one of those people played an important role in ensuring our house would be ready before we returned, and we appreciated all of them. I was told they worked almost around the clock, all in an effort to create a new start for us in a house that used to be our home; a house that needed to become a home for us once again.

So, the next morning Troy came by and picked us up. As we rode along, we made small talk about the Florida trip, but as we got close to the house, we were told we had to wear blindfolds. We obliged and joked about how this was sort of like the television show we used to watch, *Extreme Home Makeover*. On that show, they would send the family away for a few days, then bring them back to a completely remodeled house.

When we got out of Troy's truck that day, we were blindfolded, but we could hear people cheering. We were ushered to an area I assumed was directly in front of our house, then told to remove the blindfolds. When we did, I began to laugh because we were facing a school bus, which was blocking our view of the house.

If you have ever seen *Extreme Home Makeover*, you know what was next. "Move that bus!" the crowd chanted, and more cheering ensued as we finally got to see our house once again.

From just the view outside, it was immediately apparent how much work went into this project.

A new deck had been added to the front, a sidewalk from the deck to the driveway had been installed, and beautiful landscaping had been done along the sidewalk and deck, and it even stretched along the entire front of the house. It was breathtaking, to say the least. We had not even entered the house yet, and I was amazed at how much had been done in such a short time.

There was more to see, so we headed in the front door. As we entered and toured the home, we saw that the old carpet had been replaced with hardwood flooring that ran throughout the entire house. Rooms were repainted and redecorated. Long overdue repairs had been done on many items I should have done already. A new dishwasher had replaced the old one that had recently broken. It was all so special, but one of my favorite things was how they had taken drawings that Seth had done and framed them for us, hanging those special pictures on the wall by our bed. I still look at them frequently. That idea was one of pure love and an understanding of what we needed. It was absolutely perfect.

The sheer amount of work everyone did in about a five-day period was absolutely unbelievable. What touched me the most was how an entire community came together to do something so amazing. They did it because they wanted to show they cared, expressing their love and support for us through the work they did and the time they gave.

It amazes me that as bad as things seem in this world, people will still rise up and show love through their actions when tragedy strikes. I will never be able to express in full just how thankful I am for everything that was done for my family, but I will say it was the most heart-warming thing I've ever experienced. What they did has forever impacted me in a positive way, and I will never forget it. The human spirit can be amazing, and I now look for ways to pay it forward whenever I can. That's the least I can do.

Facebook Post On April 8, 2013

Tonight we are back in our home. It is going to take time to settle in, but at least we are home. Our community, family and friends all came together to remodel our house while we were gone. The house is beautiful and more important is all of the love and support that went into all of this work. We will forever be grateful for what has been done for us and this just reminds us why we live in a small town. People around here do care and our one stop light town has rallied around us like you would not believe.

It gives you light in your life when things are dark. It reminds you that the world can be beautiful when things are ugly. It gives you hope even though things may seem hopeless. Times like these show what the world could be like if we all lived our lives with love in our hearts. Our home makeover was so much more than simply a week of hard work on a house. It was love and it reminds me of Seth's love, of God's love. It was a glimpse of what good can be done for others. It was a little bit of heaven on earth at a time when a little heaven was desperately needed. In fact we have to wonder - is this what heaven will be like?

I imagine it will be better, but right now I think we will accept the fact that this world can still be the one that God envisioned when he created it. One of more love and less of everything else. At least we hope so. We thank everybody who participated in this and want to stress that as much as we love the house it is the things that I have mentioned here that we love more. This week my entire family got their Snuggle Time from a whole big group of people and tonight we rest with hope in our hearts and overflowing thanks. God Bless everyone. And to Seth - What time is it? Daddy loves you little man. So much.

CHAPTER THIRTEEN

Bumps in the Night

That night as we settled into bed, my wife and I were talking about how we were going to start over. I knew in the days, weeks, and months ahead things would likely get more difficult. I anticipated the fact that others had to go back to their own lives now. They had work, their own children, and their own families to take care of. The difficulty for us was going to be figuring out how to live without our child. What now? Things were never going to be the same.

Once we were all settled in for the night, my wife and I talked about the fact that her sister, who had been housesitting for us previously, had shared with us how there were several unusual things that had been occurring in our home. The toys in Seth's room would unexpectedly make noise. I'm sure you know how many toys are programmed to say certain things or play a certain song if the toy is pushed or moved in some manner. We were told that those types of toys would randomly go off, especially at night. Linda said a light had even come on several times around the house, and they simply had no explanation as to why. So as we lay there that first night, we were more than a bit nervous. Would we hear the sounds, too, or were all those things she claimed nothing more than the brain thinking, maybe wishing, it had heard something?

It didn't take long for us to get an answer.

As we lay there, neither one of us could sleep. It was eerily quiet, and there were a lot of various thoughts running through our minds. Soon the silence and dark made us both uneasy, so we decided we would turn on the bedroom TV. Eventually, that would become our nightly ritual. It was not a matter of us actually watching TV in bed; rather it just provided background noise to keep away the silence. Silence was no longer our friend, as it gave our brains too much opportunity to think about what we'd experienced, and neither of us really wanted that.

That particular night, I'd just started to nod off when Trish poked me. "Tim, did you hear that?" she asked.

Of course, I had not heard anything, as I'd just fallen asleep. My wife had muted the TV show she'd been watching, and she was sitting up.

"I heard something in the family room. It sounded like a thump, then someone walking across the floor," she told me.

Of course, I was skeptical, but I just sat there and supportively listened to her. At first I only heard the same silence we'd experienced before...like I said, at first.

Suddenly, I heard a loud thump and the sounds of footsteps, just like Trish had claimed. I noticed our dog was sitting up in her bed as well. Her ears were raised, her head was tilted, and she was listening to something very intently. Princess, as I have mentioned before, is a full-blooded German Shepherd, and she looks exactly like one of those police dogs you have likely seen in a movie or on TV.

As Seth grew, Princess was right there by his side. She would sleep on the floor by the crib and, eventually, at the foot of his bed. She would lay outside in the yard and watch Seth intently as he ran around and played. That dog was always keeping an alert eye on our child, her child. There was a special, undeniable bond between the two of them. So on this night, as she sat there staring at the noise we had all heard, I could not help wondering what she was thinking.

I felt a chill shoot down my spine, and if I am being honest, I felt rather scared, but I still got up and out of bed. I looked back at my wife as I put my hand on the bedroom doorknob and prepared to open the door. Her look was one of fear, and I could certainly relate to that at that very moment. I asked Princess if she wanted to come with me, but she didn't budge. She was interested in the sound but did not seem to want to leave her bed either. Thanks a lot.

I tentatively opened the door and poked my head out, not knowing what to expect. I could not make anything out in the dark, so I walked out into the family room, turned on a light, and looked around. There was nothing there, but there was certainly no denying we had heard *something*.

I took a moment to walk around the house. I checked each room. I checked on my daughter, who was sound asleep. I checked the front and back doors to make sure they were locked. I was thorough as I tried to rationalize what the sounds could have been.

I finally went back into my bedroom and told Trish there simply was not anything there. "Yes, there was," she replied with that knowing look. She mentioned how Seth always liked to jump from the couch onto the floor and would run across the room. Of course, that is the kind of thing a mom would remember, because she would be the one to keep telling him to quit doing it!

I didn't know what to think, but we had both heard it. Heck, even the dog had heard it. I decided

I wasn't going to try to explain it. Bumps and noises in the middle of the night would become something we would eventually get used to; we just weren't used to it yet.

CHAPTER FOURTEEN

Grandma was not Wrong

As we attempted to settle into a new routine, a new life, I found myself searching for answers. So much had happened, but I had not really stopped to think about it or understand it, and now I was at a point where I wanted to figure it all out.

It had to make sense, right? I mean, the world is supposed to be orderly and mathematical by nature, at least that is what I was always led to believe, but none of this made sense.

I began my search for answers by reading about child loss, but I quickly lost interest in those articles. Of course I was grieving. Obviously, I would be going through stages. Yeah, I get it. But what happens in the next life? Why did I feel like I was getting all of these signs? A person can have only so many 'coincidences' before giving in to the idea that there may be a lot more to it. A friend once said her pastor calls them "God incidences" rather than coincidences. Fair enough.

I soon found myself delving into a wide variety of different topics. One thing I stumbled upon involved hospice and several end-of-life stories. Hospice workers would recount times when there were some really interesting things occuring as people prepared to move on from this life to the next. It was fascinating.

Reading those stories took me back to the night when my own grandma died. I went to visit her in the hospital that day, and she was joyful and happy, but weak. We spent several hours talking about many different topics, and when it was time to go, I told her I would be back the next morning. What she said next shocked me.

"I won't be here in the morning," she said matter-of-factly.

I was taken aback by how blunt she had said it. It was in such a casual manner, I was not sure how to take it.

When I told her not to talk like that, she reassured me, "I've had a good life, and I've seen everyone I wanted to see except my one son. It's time to go."

I said my goodbyes once again, assuming my grandmother was wrong. There was no way she was going to leave us; however, just a few hours after I had left I received a call from my Aunt Charlene. Grandma was gone.

After the initial shock wore off, Charlene proceeded to tell me something that has stuck with me all these years regarding my grandmother's final minutes. Charlene said shortly after I left, Grandma began to fade in and out of consciousness. At one point, Charlene thought Grandma was talking to her, because she launched into a very vocal conversation.

Charlene then told me that Grandma was talking to someone, but it was someone who wasn't there, at least not someone my aunt could see. Grandma was telling the unseen person she was ready to go, and there was a back-and-forth between the two of them for several minutes. Now, my grandma was a loving and wonderful woman, but she was also a very stubborn individual, and this discussion was no different.

"What do you want me to say?" she asked. "I've said my goodbyes." Charlene retold the story in vivid detail, and it felt as if I had been there myself. Grandma continued to argue with whomever it was she was speaking with when finally she blurted out, "Yes, I love him." With that, Charlene said the conversation ended. Nothing more was said. Grandma was gone.

The one person that she had not been able to see was her son, David. I was told that Uncle

Dave had a rather difficult relationship with his mother growing up. I even heard that he spent time traveling with the circus, among doing several other things, in order to get away. I cannot speak to the accuracies of those statements as I am merely repeating things others have said, but it was something that had definitely weighed heavily on Grandma for many years, and it was during her final conversation on this Earth that she made peace with that very issue.

Many of the hospice stories I read discussed conversations like the one my grandma had, but some were even more intriguing. I found myself engrossed for hours at a time in those stories.

From there, I ended up reading about near-death experiences, which were unlike anything I had ever read before. Those stories introduced me to many concepts that I had never given much thought too. What does happen when we die?

Then came the reincarnation stories, especially the ones involving young children remembering past lives, and those piqued my interest to new levels. I never believed reincarnation was even remotely possible, and I still do not know how to feel about it, but the stories were definitely intriguing.

Of course, the idea of reincarnation is quite common in many Eastern religions, so I wanted to know more about that, and before long I found myself studying various religions from around the world. I opened my mind as I considered each religion independently, and although I'm a Christian at my core, I found that each one of those different belief systems had something positive to be taken from it.

What I learned, I should probably share in a different book, because there is way more to it than I can possibly explain here. Let's just say my eyes were opened to other possibilities as I dug deeper into my research.

Meanwhile, the signs in our home continued. Pictures would fall off the walls. The items on shelves would be moved. There were lots of unexplained bumps, thuds, and other sounds in the middle of the night. The TV would come on unexpectedly, and we would walk into a room to find the light already on. I'm not naïve, and I understand some people will truly doubt those things really happened. I know this because I was one of those people.

I rarely bought into the "things that can't be explained" concept, but now I was living it. In fact, it was becoming such a normal occurrence, I almost came to expect it. I now accept the fact that, despite what others may say, signs are real. They happen, and you can't explain them all away, no matter how hard you try.

This was illustrated to perfection one evening

as I was napping in my lounge chair in the family room. My wife was watching TV, and suddenly she woke me.

"Tim, look!" she yelled.

I was groggy from being unexpectedly awakened after just having fallen asleep, but I grudgingly looked at what she was pointing at: The ceiling fan was slowly turning. Feeling a bit grouchy, I questioned why she found a rotating ceiling fan so impressive.

She then pointed to the light switch, "See, it's off."

She was correct. The light switch *was* off. Well, I patiently explained to her, an electrical current can still get through if the switch is not connected properly, and even a slight draft could cause the blades of the fan to move. Logical. Scientific. Simple.

As I was in the midst of stating my thought pattern, the fan came to a stop. "There you go," I said.

I thought that was the end of it, but then the fan began to move again. This time, it turned in the opposite direction and began to move at a fairly rapid pace. I sat there, dumbfounded, as Trish smiled.

"Told you." She was so smug.

Regardless of how hard I tried to explain logically what I'd just witnessed, I could not. Maybe there's a science wiz or electrical expert out there who could give me some insight, because I hate to admit that my wife was right. I cannot explain it. It seemed to be yet another sign in an endless supply as of late.

CHAPTER FIFTEEN

The Dream

One night, after a particularly trying day emotionally, I went to lay down for bed. It did not take long there for me to drift off to sleep; however, this night was much different from the ones I normally had. On this night, I experienced a dream so vivid and real, it felt like I was not asleep at all.

I recall that I was standing at a high school baseball field, watching the kids play a game. I could smell the freshly cut grass. I could feel the sun shining down, as well as a light breeze blowing from behind me.

The pitcher delivered the ball, and the batter swung and missed. "Strike!" yelled the umpire.

As I watched the game, I felt something pulling at me. It was hard to explain, but I somehow knew I needed to take a walk and so I began to head towards a road located just beyond left field. As I approached the road, the sounds of the game began to fade. As unusual as that was, I just kept walking, and soon I was crossing over.

When I say, "crossing over," I meant the road, but in hindsight I was crossing over a lot more than I realized in that moment, because as soon as I crossed the road, the light began to fade and a darkness set in. The sounds of the baseball game quickly dissipated, and soon there was only silence. I was surrounded by nothing but the dark now, and an eerie quiet.

I kept walking, and before long I could sense others around me. I could not see anything, as it was still pitch black, but I could literally feel the presence of something in the dark. A voice called out. I could not make out what it said, but it did not sound friendly. Soon, I was hearing a lot of voices, and I am not ashamed to say I was feeling more than just a little frightened.

The voices were saying mean and disgusting things. Some words seemed to be directed towards me, but the majority seemed as if they were being said to others in the dark. I heard what sounded like fighting, and it seemed as if punches were being thrown. I then heard what sounded like thuds, and some voices called out in pain, while others laughed. Because I was still blind in the darkness, I can't say for certain what I was experiencing, but I was obviously in the midst of a violent area of some type.

I felt hands grab my shirt and yank, while another voice told me to follow it. Before I had a chance to react, I felt more hands and more voices were calling to me. I began to twist and turn, fighting to get loose. I started yelling for them to leave me alone, and as soon as I broke free, I ran as fast as I could.

I was unsure where I was running to or if I might trip over something, but the fear made me just keep running as fast as I could. The voices began to fade, and it did not feel like I was being followed, but I kept on running - then suddenly, and unexpectedly, I emerged into the light. The shock of going from complete blackness into a brightly lit place caused me to stop and stumble, and before I realized it, I was lying on the ground, waiting for my eyes to adjust to the light.

When I was able to see once again, I realized I was in some type of old town. It's hard to describe; the best way I can explain it is to say it reminded me of one of those small towns where stores and businesses lined both sides of the street. I should say it was more like one of those old western towns from the movies. The road I was sitting on was made of dirt and it was certainly not a place I was familiar with.

As I stood up and brushed myself off, I finally realized there were people standing along both sides of the street. I saw people of all walks of life. They were different ages, sizes, and appeared to come from different backgrounds. As I slowly walked along the street, it felt sort of like they were all expecting a parade. Everyone just stood there, patiently waiting, and no one seemed to pay me any attention.

I continued scanning the crowd and realized something was happening directly in front of me on the street. Before I knew what was going on, a black hole opened just a few feet off the ground, and suddenly a young man stepped out of it. I heard the crowd let out a roar of approval, cheering and yelling. A man and woman came running towards the young man, and soon they were hugging.

I was shocked, to say the least, but I made my way around them and continued along. What exactly was that all about? I wondered if I had somehow opened a portal from the dark place I had been in and now others were able to escape, like I had done.

It did not take long before another hole opened, another person stepped out, and another excited cheer from the crowd rang out. This pattern repeated itself over and over again, with happy people eagerly welcoming those who they apparently loved. As those around me celebrated, I found myself focusing on finding Seth. I somehow knew he was there, and I felt like he was close.

As I began to run down the street, I started calling for him while my eyes frantically searched the crowd; however, as I reached the end of the road, I began to think I was wrong - and that was when he came walking around the corner. He looked so happy, healthy, and vibrant.

"I'm right here, Dad," he said, so nonchalant. It was sort of like saying, *Where else would I be?*

I picked up my son, gave him a gigantic hug, then I was abruplty jolted awake. I shot up in bed, looking around; the bedroom was quiet and still dark. I lay back down, frustrated. I wanted nothing more in the world than just to be able to go back to that very moment. It may have been a dream, but it seemed like so much more.

I could remember every detail, every smell, every single moment. That dream was far different from any other I'd ever had. It was so vivid and intense, it made me question exactly what I had just experienced. To be quite honest, I have no adequate words to express my thoughts on the subject. It just seemed as if it was more than just a dream, but even now I can't explain what I experienced. Was it just a dream? Or was it something more?

CHAPTER SIXTEEN

My Cousin Has Smart Kids

T he end of April came around, and we were still struggling, but I decided it would be good to have a few family and friends over to our home for my wife's birthday. It was nothing big, but it was nice to host something positive for a change.

We had a nice time visiting and talking with everyone, then something interesting happened. As I stood in the kitchen, talking to my cousin, her young son came in from outside. He looked tired and very grouchy. As his mother tried to reason with him, he was having none of it. I had been there once or twice and knew all about this kind of behavior.

As I watched their exchange, I felt very jealous that she had the opportunity to try to console her child. As I thought about it, I realized I had never gotten upset with Seth when he acted like that. I'm not saying those were joyous moments, but some people get mad at their kids because they get frustrated themselves. Normally, I was able to reason with him...eventually. At least that is the way that I was remembering it now.

Anyways, my cousin handled her son very well and knew exactly how to talk with him, yet despite her best efforts, I could see he was not going to be easily swayed.

Then it happened. Something told me to step in, so I asked him if he wanted to play with some of Seth's toys. He told me no, but when I told him he could play with Seth's cars, he quickly changed his mind.

I led him back to what would soon be my office, and we pulled out Seth's toy cars. I had already forgotten how many of them we'd accumulated over the years! I sat on the floor, and together we began rummaging through them. He would tell me which cars either he or his other cousins had, then show them to me. I would tell him which ones Seth liked best, then show them to him.

Someone came in to check on us and asked me if I was alright, to which I replied simply, "Yeah, I'm fine."

You see, this was a big moment for me, and everyone knew it. Ever since Seth died, I had not been able to be around boys close to his age. I could handle girls, but around the boys I would break, the tears would flow, a sick feeling would overcome me, and I would have to walk away. This time, it was different. This time, I felt a sense of peace and a hand on my shoulder, guiding me.

The cars soon gave way to him going through the little box of toys I had in the room, and we discussed how both he and Seth liked Transformers. He saw the bigger Transformer toys on the shelf, and before I had time to object, he was suddenly pulling them off to play with them.

For a brief second, I cringed because the shelves had all the toys Seth liked to play with a lot. The entire room was sort of a cross between an office and things from my son's room. The things on the shelf were not meant to be played with, yet they were. They were toys; they were *not* Seth. That first few seconds of me being unsure quickly gave way to us playing Transformers together, just like Seth and I had done numerous times before.

I didn't feel sad at that moment in time. I actually felt relieved in some weird way. It was like another heavy burden had been lifted off me, like Seth was alive and with me yet again.

Later that evening, I was sitting on the porch, talking with a few of the other parents, when my cousin's older son, Collin, sat down on my lap and asked me to help him with a game he was playing on his iPad. Collin was around seven years old at the time, so he, too, was rather close to Seth's age, and it was yet another moment that reminded me of my own child. Seth would crawl up on my lap and ask me to help him with his games fairly regularly. I think sometimes he needed help, but most of the time it was just another moment to snuggle up, and he liked feeling close like that.

As I assisted Collin with his game, I also continued to talk with the other adults. At one point, I made the comment, "Well, since Seth died..."

Without ever looking up from his game, little Collin said, "Seth's not dead. He went to Heaven, and now he lives there, but he's not dead."

My heart melted, and I told him he was right. I guess my cousin just has smart kids.

CHAPTER SEVENTEEN

Mother's Day

E very first without your loved one is painful in ways that are hard to explain. That's just a fact, and there is no way around it.

I shuddered when Mother's Day approached, fully realizing how difficult the day would be for my wife. I was not wrong. Trish had already been depressed since the accident, as we all had, but Mother's Day amplified that feeling a hundredfold for her. I had no comforting words, no way to help her. All I could do was be there to hold her, listen to her, and cry with her.

When the day finally came, our family and friends checked in, and we managed to spend time with a few people we loved. We then stopped by Seth's grave so Trish could take a moment to be with the one child she had not had a chance to be with yet.

It weighs heavy on my heart knowing many people out there go through this kind of difficulty on holidays, but I am actually going to share with you something positing; how Trish's day was brightened a little more than expected.

We pulled into the cemetery and parked near Seth's grave site. I let out a deep breath as we opened the car doors and we slowly made our way towards the headstone just a few feeet away. As we approached Seth's lot, I was surprised to see a card and single flower lying there.

The card was addressed to Trish, and it contained one of the sweetest notes, wishing her well and thanking her for being "a great momma" not only to her kids, but to many others as well. It went on, saying they hoped her day was as good as it could be. The card was not signed.

I watched my wife's reaction and saw the way that card moved her. It was a deep and emotional reaction that I witnessed her have. I realized by not signing it, the person who had left it had made the moment even more special because my wife began to think back to all of the many kids that she had helped over the years. As she was trying to figure out who it was that left the card she was now enjoying many fond memories that had been created along the way.

I must say, I wish I could be as thoughtful, caring, and full of love as the person who did that must be. To have the mindset to think of others in such a meaningful way, then take it to another entire level by actually getting a card, a flower, and writing such a precious note - it was all so amazing. So, to the anonymous person who did this, please know you are special in ways many of us are not. Whoever you may be, I admire you for caring and showing such love and compassion for others.

Now, imagine how much better the world would be if all of us did things like this for others. That moment served as another reminder that I need to continue to grow, because I can tell you, I'm not anywhere near as thoughtful as that person is. I wish I was.

CHAPTER EIGHTEEN

Baseball & Rainbows

The first official night of baseball started for our local youth league in May. It was bittersweet as expected, and as the Little League team that I was helping Troy coach played on the front field, I couldn't help glancing to the backfield, where Seth's t-ball team was playing their first game as well. Ever since that morning, I had been feeling down, and I didn't know why. It just reminded me a lot of those first few days after Seth died.

It surprised me how quickly those pains could come back, but again, I didn't know why they all had suddenly came flooding back. It never crossed my mind that the reason might be because it was our area's first official day of baseball, and it would have been Seth's first chance to play on a real team.

I made it through the games, and both Seth's t-ball team and our Little League team got their wins. However, I noticed a few things about me are different now. For one, I seem to have much more patience for the mistakes the kids make when playing the game. I mean, we still have to be disciplined and try to teach the fundamentals, the meaning of hard work, good teamwork, and all those things, but now I don't find myself getting worked up over the little things. A missed ground ball, a bad throw, etc. is all just part of a game the kids are playing.

That's a big thing for me, because everyone who knows me personally knows I have always been super competitive in everything I've done. I like to win. It's probably not a great trait, but winning is something a lot of us like. Regardless whether I was playing or if I was coaching, I've always been super competitive; yet even though I wanted to win that night, it didn't seem as important anymore. Having fun, teaching the kids, and giving our best was.

After the game, as I addressed the team, I stressed to them the importance of getting better in certain areas, but I also stressed it was important that they just enjoy the win, enjoy the fact that they got to play this great game, and enjoy being with each other. To be honest, this was all new for me; just enjoying each moment for what it is and not worrying about the little things.

I'm not sure what the future holds, but I think I may end up being a better coach and better person in the end. Of course, don't think that means I won't be competitive when it matters! I'll always have some of that, but I think it just means I won't sweat those little mistakes like I used to.

Facebook Post: May 12, 2013

"Yesterday we were in Cardington, taking photos of their baseball teams. We always look forward to taking photos of our friends and their kids. While the day started out as many others have...it ended a bit bittersweet! The last team of the day was the team that Tim Maceyko is a coach of. As Rick was setting up the team photo...I was talking old times with Tim. On the field behind us, Tim noticed a cardinal that had just landed on the pitcher's mound! While Seth was not there with us...he was there with us. I must say, the experience is hard to express in words." – Jen Tackett

A few days later I was standing at the baseball field, preparing for practice, when Matt Meyers approached me. Matt was helping us coach, and he was also a father of one of the kids on this year's team. Matt was also a sheriff's deputy and just an all-around good guy. He looked at me with a serious look on his face, took a breath, and then said what was on his mind.

"I wanted to wait until things settled down before I told you this, but I saw the most amazing things at your house on that night."

I looked at Matt with what came across as a puzzled expression I'm sure because I quickly realized "that night" was *that night.*

Matt proceeded to tell me how he was driving by my home the night of the accident and heard something come across his radio, but he wasn't actually working, so he did not realize what was actually going on at that particular moment. As he drove on by our residence, he looked over and said it was literally snowing in our back yard and a beautiful rainbow stretched across the sky directly behind the house. He said he wasn't sure where it ended but said it looked like it was landing right in the back yard.

The sight was surreal for Matt, and he was awestruck by the beauty of it all, but other than thinking it was a pretty cool view to behold, he didn't give it much thought - at least not until he heard what had happened. After learning the news, he couldn't help thinking about what he had seen over and over again. He told me that he had wanted to share it with me for quite some time but was afraid of how it might seem.

However, after everything I had been experiencing, there was absolutely nothing about his story that struck me as unusual. It was just one more thing I simply could not explain, just one more thing some people would write off as another coincidence. Yet you have to wonder: How many coincidences can a person have before there's something to it all?

I thanked Matt for sharing, smiled, and chalked it up to just another one of the many things I was never going to be able to explain.

Ezekiel 1:28 (KJV) states: "As the appearance of the bow that is in the cloud in the day of rain, so was the appearance of the likeness of the glory of the LORD. And when I saw, I fell upon my face, and I heard a voice of one that spake."

I realize it takes certain weather conditions for a rainbow to appear, but with my experiences with the weather, I firmly believe that God controls it; so, every time I see a rainbow now, I look at it a little longer and a little more intensely.

Do rainbows have more meaning than we will ever understand? That's hard to say, but I'm not beyond connecting the dots and considering every possibility these days. Either way, I'll never view the beauty of a rainbow again without thinking about that spring day in 2013.

CHAPTER NINETEEN

Dear Dad Who Lost

One morning, I was having an extremely difficult time getting out of bed. I cried in the shower yet again, then slowly and reluctantly prepared to go to work.

Some days are just like that; after losing a child, deep depression can set in. However, I still had a family to support and a mortgage to pay, so I had no other choice than just to get up and go. On this particular morning though, it was especially hard.

When I walked out the front door of the house, I heard the call. The cardinal's call. I walked around the corner of the house and looked into the back yard. There, perched high in a tree, sat the bright red bird. He was singing his song and calling out over and over again.

His sounds soothed my soul at that moment,

filling me with a sense of happiness. I just stood there listening for several minutes, then I finally had to pull myself away and get in my vehicle to head to work.

As I drove towards the office, a bird flew across the front of my car. I laughed because it, too, was a cardinal. I suddenly didn't feel as depressed after that second cardinal appeared. In fact, those feelings were replaced by new thoughts.

I thought about how I was still being spoken to and someone was still listening to my pain. I had long given up not believing in the signs and allowed these moments to give me a "faith boost", as I liked to call it. I know each of us can use a "faith boost" every now and then and the cardinal seemed to now officially be mine!

The days continued to come and go. Some were good and some were bad. And suddenly, it was Father's Day. Like Mother's Day, it was as horrible a holiday as one would imagine it would be for me. There was nothing that could make the day OK.

It was my turn to feel the pain ratchet up. Each holiday brings memories, smiles, and a lot of heartache, missing what you no longer have. It's inevitable and expected, but that does not make it any easier.

I thought about how I now had a unique perspective on Father's Day. It's a view not everyone has, so I wanted to let other dads know someone else understands their pain.

Fact: Most dads who have lost a child will suffer in silence. They are the man of the house, and they lead. They stay strong. They don't typically talk about what they are feeling, and they likely do not go to counseling. Maybe we should, but that's the way it is.

It was with these thoughts in mind that I sat down one day and wrote a letter for fathers everywhere who suffer in silence. It was my hope that maybe my words could help someone. Maybe by including it in this book, it will.

Dear Dad Who Lost

I know how you feel. I understand. A dad is supposed to protect. A dad cares for his family. He provides comfort, leadership and discipline. He supports, teaches, and loves. He's the first man his daughter admires, and he's the guy his son wants to be. He's dad, one of the most powerful things a man can be.

It's more powerful than any amount of money you can make. It's more powerful than any job you can have. It's more powerful and more amazing than any house you can own. It's even way cooler than any car you could ever drive. In reality, there is no comparison; Dad is dad, and he's 'the man'.

So, when you lose a child, you question everything you are, everything you think, everything you're supposed to be.

Why couldn't I stop this? What could I have done differently? Did I do everything possible, or did I fail to make the world safe for my baby? Why would God do this to my family? Why? Why? Why?

The questions are endless, and the answers are few. I know because I've been there. I understand.

I've stared into space for hours. I've cried in the shower many mornings. I've fallen to my knees, unable to take the pain. I've lashed out at those I love. I've spent endless amounts of time alone, trying to avoid others. And I've stayed as busy as I can to avoid dealing with those thoughts, those feelings. No matter how much time passes, I think that will always be my favorite way to deal with it. Staying busy lets you ignore the hurt buried inside. My point here is that it's normal. It's part of the process. I get it.

Now, I don't have all the answers, but I can tell you this: You may not be able to see it now, but everything truly does happen for a reason. It may not make sense at this moment, and you may be on your knees right now, but believe me when I say, keep your eyes wide open. Watch for the signs, keep the faith, and hold those around you tight. They need it, and so do you.

Love is what will get you through, and love is what will show you the way going forward. There are days and moments when I still question and ask why, but we have to believe and stay strong. We have to hope because hope is the one thing we have. The hope that if we make something positive out of this, then one day we will see our child again, when the time is right.

Then everything will make sense. Hold on to that on those nights when the world gets a little dark. Let that thought provide you a little light when you need it the most. Keep the faith.

It does get easier in some ways with time, although you are forever changed. The way you feel. The way you think. The way you view the world. It's all different. *You* are different. That's the way it is. But that doesn't mean it's over. Look for that new path now. Don't be afraid to have faith and walk down a different road than the one you were walking before. There is still beauty in this world, and you are here for a reason. Find it. Watch for it. And make it mean something.

So to all those dads who have lost, I understand. I've been there. I *am* there. I wish you all the best, and I realize how difficult Father's Day can be. There are no words for any of you that can take away the pain. I'm sorry you belong to this club, but keep the faith. You are strong. You are Dad.

CHAPTER TWENTY

Jeff & Seth

Facebook Post July 24, 2013

Thanks to Jeff Dunham's publicist, Trish and I will be heading to the Ohio State Fair tonight to see Jeff in concert. He is my wife's favorite comedian - she loves Peanut and the puppets - so she is really excited. However, there are mixed emotions since the fair was always a Seth thing. I guess you just take the good with the bad in life. As for me, I'm looking forward to a night of laughs and fun. There haven't been many of those lately so sending out a special thank you to Jeff Dunham's people.

As the middle of July rolled around, I continued to be concerned about my wife. The things she had experienced were still giving her night terrors, and her depressed state made for long, difficult days. I needed to do something to help her, in some way. It was around that time when I realized her favorite comedian and ventriloquist, Jeff Dunham, was coming to the Ohio State Fair.

I had decided I would purchase tickets and try to see if we couldn't escape the world for an evening. As I looked around online the thought hit me that I should reach out to Jeff's publicist, explain our situation, and see if there was any possibility of my wife meeting him. I figured it would be an unexpected treat for her and it would certainly be something she would never forget. So, I wrote an email and pressed 'send'.

Unfortunately, when I received a response, I was told a meeting was not going to be possible, but then I was pleasantly surprised when we were offered complimentary tickets to the show. Of course, I graciously accepted and later shocked my wife with the news.

On July 24th, we made the one-hour trip from our home to the Columbus Fairgrounds. During the drive, my wife and I made small talk about the upcoming show. She was really excited to see Peanut and the many other characters Jeff would present, but she also made it clear she was dreading the idea of going to the fair itself.

A fair is something you tend to enjoy with your family, with your kids - and boy, did Seth enjoy the fair! The animals, the rides, the games, and even the food. Of course, as parents you enjoy seeing the joy on your child's face, and despite the amount of money we all end up spending, it is truly great quality time together.

As we walked through the fair entrance, I held my wife's hand, and right away I could tell how uncomfortable she was. Knowing how she was feeling, I made sure we made our way directly to the building where the show would be held.

There was no walking around and no fair food. I ensured there was minimal risk of us seeing the many happy families with the smiling children. This fair trip was all about getting into the show to enjoy ourselves, so it was a straight line to the front doors and into the building. No tears tonight!

We picked up our tickets at the front window and made our way into the venue a little early. Surprisingly, other people were already inside, and we stood looking around, not sure where exactly we were supposed to go. A young man serving as an usher approached and asked if we needed help. Upon showing him our tickets, he pointed out our seats and tried to explain where they were.

Unexpectedly, he suddenly decided it would be easier just to walk us to them. He chatted us up as we walked along, then commented about how awesome our seats were. It turned out we were ten rows back on the floor and right dead in the center. The seats were perfect and better than we ever could have expected.

We thanked the young man for the brief conversation and for his help. We then sat down in our seats as he walked away. Trish looked at me with a big smile and asked if I had seen his name tag. Indeed I had. We had been seated by "Seth" for the show.

The night could not have turned out to better. Jeff Dunham put on an incredible show, and we enjoyed ourselves immensely. We laughed so hard, both of us complained that our faces hurt. It was good to feel happy again, even if it was short-term. It was simply an amazing night, and somehow Seth had managed to be a part of it.

CHAPTER TWENTY-ONE

Searching for Hope

The summer snuck by and it was not long before the month of August was coming to an end. Of course that also meant that it was now time for the local county fair. In our area it always runs the week before Labor Day, and this year I had reached out to the fair board to discuss holding a small event as part of the fair itself. There had been a rash of recent losses the past several months in our area, and it seemed like a memorial service for all those who had been suffering seemed appropriate.

I had begun to realize that, despite my own pain, there were a lot of people out there suffering, too, and they needed the same kind of support we had been receiving. Holding a tribute service seemed like a good way to honor those who had recently passed and show people others cared.

So I stood on a small stage at the fair that week in August and led a service that we had named, "Dancing in the Sky." The event name actually came from a beautiful song sung by a duo named Dani and Lizzy. Their song, "Dancing in the Sky" encompasses so many things that many of us are feeling after losing someone that we loved. From the moment I first heard it I knew that it would help a lot of people by through the meaningful and impactful lyrics. If you have not heard it I highly recommend that you do a quick search on the internet for it. And you may want to have the tissues nearby.

During the service pastors spoke, singers sang, and we had a moment of sharing with audience members, saying the names of those they had lost. That was a truly special moment, and a deeply touching moment for me personally. Many people, many names, much suffering, and tons of people supporting one another.

We were also blessed to have author Kevin Malarkey speak. Kevin wrote *The Boy Who Came Back from Heaven*, and his speech was inspiring. His words gave those in attendance a lot of hope, and there were several tears as he spoke.

At the conclusion of his speech, Kevin gave out free copies of his book and spent time talking to the many people who waited patiently in line to meet him. I should also mention Mr. Malarkey not only gave out free, signed copies of his book, he did not charge us anything to come speak at our event. He later told me, "I still have my child, so to hear these stories, it touches my soul."

Later on, things took a difficult turn for him when Kevin's son claimed the things he had written in their book were not true. The publisher eventually pulled the book, and the story made national headlines as people called Kevin a fraud. It was all incredibly shocking, as that narrative just did not seem to fit the guy I had met.

I reached out by email to Kevin and asked him how he was doing and expressed how surprised I was by the recent turn of events. His response was simply that he did not understand why his wife was saying what she was and that he still stood by what he had written originally. He did not comment on why his son changed his story, and I did not press, but I could tell he was pained by the entire situation and he seemed to still believe in what had been written.

I took the time to do a quick search and found that Kevin's wife, Beth, had been claiming the book had inaccuracies for quite some time. It appeared that Kevin and Beth had gone through a difficult, strained relationship over the topic. My understanding is that she had never truly agreed with the book and felt not only was it inaccurate, it was also a misrepresentation of what their son had experienced.

I have no idea what the exact facts are behind all those things, as well as who is right or who is wrong; nor I do think it is my place to judge either of them, but the entire situation made me put a lot more thought into the many Heaven-related books that have been so popular. After losing Seth, I initally read as many of them as I could find.

In fact, I had already or would eventually finish *Heaven is for Real, 90 Minutes in Heaven, Proof of Heaven, Waking Up in Heaven,* and a several others. After digesting all that, I came to my own conclusion about the stories and how I look at them.

So what are my thoughts? Well, what I will say is that I disagree with people who are telling others to stop reading these kinds of books. I disagree with people who say the stories are dangerous because they aren't Biblically accurate. I disagree with anyone who tries to suppress others from reading them, but *why* do I feel that way? My position is very simple actually. I disagree because those books give people hope.

Because of those books, I found some strength to keep fighting, keep trying. There are so many dark days and difficult moments after a loss. Sometimes you feel as if you just don't have the power to keep going. Sometimes you're not even sure you want to. Yet, during those exact moments, I would pick up one of those books and escape into another world for a little while.

I would escape to a world where hope was abundant. A world where my personal pain did not exist. A world where love and the concept of a happy ending was all-encompassing. I was never being brainwashed by what I read, and I didn't take many things as seriously as maybe the writer actually intended. What I did take from each one of those stories was the fact that even when life seems to be at its worst, there is still a chance. There is still some light. There is still hope.

And that is what we all need when we are at the lowest points in our lives. We need hope when life has dealt us a bad hand and we are not sure how we are going to deal with it. We need hope when we don't know how to get back up after being knocked down. Life can be tough, and it is that little glimmer of light that allows us to have some faith. Faith means maybe we can somehow still make it.

That's what I took from all those books. I totally and completely understand why some people want nothing to do with them, and that's OK, but I do believe there is a reason that the books are as popular as they are. Now, I do not think people should automatically believe every detail written, but I do think many people out there are just like me. They are looking for anything that can lift their spirits, anything that can give them a level of confidence that they can make it.

I actually hope that is what this book does for people as well. I didn't go to Heaven, so I can't speak about how that may or may not be. My son didn't die and come back either; he just died. He left, and that's my reality. That's my life. That's as real as it gets.

However, that doesn't mean I shouldn't have hope. That doesn't mean I don't have faith. And it doesn't mean God abandoned me. I think he's been talking to me this entire time and I've just been lucky enough to take notice of some of the amazing things around me.

I strongly believe He talks to all of us. So, why don't we all see it? Why don't we hear it? Normally, we're so busy in our lives that we fail to stop long enough to notice anything! Life is so fast-paced, and we're so concerned with worldly things that we fail to see what's right in front of us. Other times, we're caught up in our pain and we don't see much of anything. I get it. I'm just as guilty.

But let me ask you: Have you ever taken a walk in the woods? It is one of the most beautiful experiences on this planet. When we escape the cell phones, social media, work, and hustle and bustle of the world and reconnect with nature, it is nothing short of amazing.

I believe when we face something traumatic, our eyes are opened and our ears are listening more than ever. It is in these moments that we begin to notice things we never did before. That is when we have the chance to see and hear the signs all around us. Of course, that's also when God knows that we need them, and him, the most.

So I want to challenge you to slow down this week for a little while. Turn off that cell phone, that TV, and just ignore the outside world for a while. Take a few moments to reconnect with the beauty of nature and think about those who may no longer be here with you. Remember the joyous moments, the love you shared, and the things you enjoyed with them. Consciously be aware of the things around you and see what happens.

If you believe in God and an after-life, then it's not so farfetched to believe our lost loved ones can somehow communicate with us through nature. If not them, then at the very least, it's God allowing us to know they're alright.

How that is done is beyond me, but I don't think I need to understand it. I don't think I'm necessarily supposed to understand it. I think I just need to have faith and hold on to the belief that there's something much better out there than what my human mind can understand.

I also believe I am supposed to remind others to keep an open mind. Remind them to be very aware of their surroundings, because it is possible their loved ones have already tried to communicate with them. I also need to remind others that we are not necessarily meant to understand everything today, but one day we will.

Finally, I think I need to remind myself that even though Seth is gone and my life may seem difficult, he is still here. He lives on by my thoughts, my actions, and how I love others. How I live going forward matters and that is how we honor those we've lost - the way we live going forward.

The question remains, are signs sent directly by God? Are they sent by His messengers? Or are our loved ones able to reach us after they have left? I cannot answer those questions with absolute certainty. All I know is that I feel stronger every time I see and hear the cardinals, and that's enough for me.

CHAPTER TWENTY-TWO

Love Thy Neighbor

I realized that, beyond the holidays, there would be two times of the year when the emotions of not having Seth with us would take its biggest toll. The month of his death, obviously, but also the month of his birth.

As such, November is a very emotional month, as it reminds us of what we no longer have, but it took on an even bigger meaning in 2014. On November 14th of that year, we not only celebrated another birthday without Seth, we also buried a family friend.

Actually, within just a few weeks of each other we saw not just one, but two family friends leave us long before their time was due when they each committed suicide. In one case, the family lost a wife and mother. In the other case, a husband and father. In both instances, they left behind young children.

Just like when Seth was taken, I had a difficult time understanding the why of it. I think that can be the toughest part of these moments. Why do these things happen? Sometimes the answer just isn't as obvious. My heart hurt for both families so much, and there was nothing I could do.

Upon the shocking news of Bryon's death, my family made our way over to the place where everyone was gathering. A small town like ours has a lot of common friends, and I looked around the room that day to see many of the same faces that had been there for us not so long ago.

I thought back to that time and how my wife would not initially eat. She refused everyone's attempts and expressed no interest in food. Yet her friend, Heather Deskins, finally broke through and was the first person to get Trish to finally give in and eat something. Now as I watched Heather sitting at the table, struggling with the loss of her husband, it was Trish who got Heather to eat.

I couldn't help thinking how quickly life changes for all of us. It wasn't that long ago when these two friends were in reverse roles, and now it was us who needed to be there to support and love a family in their time of need, just like they did for us.

That week, I couldn't sleep as I thought about

those kids, now without a father. I thought about Heather's pain and the family's suffering. It was horrible, and I related to what they were going to have to deal with in the coming days, weeks, and months.

However, there was one train of thought my mind seemed to keep going back to. Much like the Snuggle Time message came to me after Seth died, I kept having certain thoughts. This time, those thoughts related to Bryon and how he was full of love. So, one day I sat down and wrote the following:

Love Thy Neighbor

The Bible says, "Love Thy Neighbor," but I wonder how many of us really do that. We may see a friend or acquaintance, and of course we ask, "How are you?" But how many times do we mean it? The phrase "How are you?" has become nothing more than a simple "Hello." It's an accepted form of a generalized greeting, but how many times do we actually sit down with someone and ask, "How *are* you? What's going on in your life? Are there any problems you want to share with me? Can I help carry some of your burden for you today?"

Most of us don't because we simpy never think of it. We get so caught up in our own personal struggles, our finances, our family problems, and our work issues that we forget how to "Love Thy

Neighbor" the way God intended.

Some will say, "I shovel my neighbor's walk every winter" or "I take home-baked goods to my neighbors every Christmas", and those things are wonderful and kind, but do you really *know* your neighbors? Are they struggling with something you could help with? Are they fighting a personal battle that's weighing heavily on their minds? Most of us have no idea what's going on with our family, our friends, or our neighbors.

My friends both dying so suddenly opened my eyes to the fact that I've personally done a poor job of truly getting to know who they were on the inside and what kind of pain they may have been facing. How can any of us "love" another person if we don't really know that person? This applies literally not only to your neighbors, but also everyone in our lives.

What about that co-worker or long distance cousin? How many times have we taken the time to ask about their struggles? How often do we ask if there's any way we can help? Have you ever sat down and said, "I know you're likely hurting because life is hard, and I want you to know you're loved."

Have we, as a society, forgotten how to "Love Thy Neighbor?" Now, I'm not saying asking these questions will change anything, because there's no way we can know that. However, what I do know is that not asking these questions guarantees that nothing will change.

On the first Christmas after Seth died, Bryon wrote me a message I'll forever cherish. He often sent me texts or emails, telling me how he was thinking about Seth and my family. It became something I truly looked forward to and appreciated.

Many people went back to their lives after a few months passed, but Bryon never forgot about Seth or us. He wore his red Seth James Maceyko bracelet every day, and he made sure he checked in on us. *That* is how you "Love Thy Neighbor." Bryon was full of love and grace. When it came to the concept of loving thy neighbor, he was a better man than I.

Here's the message that Bryon sent me Christmas morning, December 25, 2013:

"Had trouble sleeping last night, a lot of things on my mind, one of them was your family. I have no words of comfort, just prayers that I keep your family in.

"As I was watching my girls open their gifts, my heart started to sink because I know a family with one less. I think of Seth often in the sun-filled days and cool autumn breeze. I think of him when the snow begins to fall and the joy he brings. I'm not wanting you to feel sad, just wanting you to know your family is on my mind and in my heart.

"This is the best way for me to tell you how I feel for your family. I know I really don't talk much in public. This is the only way I can really try to express my feelings without stumbling over myself."

I recall replying to his message and thanking Bryon for caring so much, and for being such a great friend. I also remember getting caught up in his beautiful words about my son. However, there's something I didn't do. I didn't ask him why he "had trouble sleeping last night" or what exactly was on his mind. I was busy battling with my own demons, and although I cherished his love and concern for my family, at no time did I ever consider that my friend was also battling demons himself.

In hindsight, I would give anything to be able to ask him those questions, to get to know his personal struggles and help carry his burdens for him. Obviously, it's easy to look back and think that way now, but that's what I wish.

However, I'm not sure we should be concerned with what we've done or haven't done in our past. Instead, I believe we need to ask, who do we become as a result of a tragedy like this? That's the question each of us must answer throughout our lives.

We all have a choice. We can take moments like these and become a better person, or we can say how sad it is and leave it at that. I'd like to become a better person, and I hope I do. I know it won't be easy, but if I can change just a little bit and think to ask those around me how they're doing, then that's an improvement.

If I become a better listener, then Bryon's death has some type of meaning. Seth's Snuggle Time message addressed the love between a parent and their child. Bryon's message is about building that same kind of relationship, but with other adults in our lives. Two tragic deaths, followed by two messages of love, and it's my hope that, in both cases, they help others live better lives through the love they showed us all while they were here.

CHAPTER TWENTY-THREE

The Signs

Some people believe life is black and white. It's right or wrong. It's left or right. However, after all of the things I've experienced, I've come to believe there's a lot more gray area than most of us realize. Scholars say science is strictly fact-based, and I used to be the kind of guy who needed everything to be proven. Blind faith did not come easily for me. Show me the math. Back it up with science. However, these days I would not be so quick to doubt alternative views or other ways of thinking. There is much more to all of this than I ever realized.

In this book, I have shared with you a journey that started several years ago. It is a journey no parent wants to take, but it is one many must live, and my heart aches for each of you walking that walk. Losing anyone you love can be excruciating, and I have found child loss is the worst of the worst. Writing this book was extremely difficult and, at times, very painful. Thinking back to those days and reliving those moments caused many tears as I struggled to put this together, but my hope is that by sharing it, people can understand there is much more in store for us than what our human minds can comprehend. One day, all our questions will have answers. Until then, we all have to learn to overcome adversity and make the most of this life we have been given.

Some people believe our loved ones will let us know they are alright after they leave us. Many of those believers are adamant that our loved ones do this through various means, including signs. Of course, there are also those who doubt something like that is possible in any way. I'll let you decide for yourself which camp you fall into.

As for me, I believe anything is possible, and if our eyes are open wide, then we may very well notice something that gives us strength during those darkest of days. Maybe that's because God allows it. Maybe it's because our loved ones really can reach out. Maybe there are other reasons we can't understand yet, but at the end of the day, if you can find that hope and a sense of meaning, does it really matter where it comes from? I'm willing to bet you'll take it regardless!

I'm now going to share with you several of the ways they claim our loved ones can contact us.

Maybe you've experienced some of these things, maybe not. I know I've been blessed to experience many signs along the way and I like to think that even if it is not actually Seth reaching out to me, then it is, at the very least, God providing me comfort right when I need it the most.

Dreams

Earlier, I shared a dream I had that seemed much different than most others. It was intense and seemed so real, so when I found out dreams may mean something spiritually, my interest was immediately piqued.

They say one of the most common ways for spirits to visit us is by coming through our dreams. When we're sleeping, our conscious mind has entered into a state of rest, things are quiet, and we're much more receptive to outside messages. Some people claim spirits, and even angels, can give you messages during this time.

It's highly recommended that you keep a dream journal by your bedside. Something as simple as a pad of paper with a pen on the nightstand will suffice (or your smart phone if you're like me). Regardless, the idea is that you can easily write things down when you're woken after a dream. You will want to capture as much as you can while it's fresh in your mind, because you're likely to forget certain details rather quickly.

It's quite common for people to overlook the

significance of a dream. They may also try to convince themselves a dream was "just a dream", and nothing more. Unfortunately, when we do this, we may miss out on a powerful message we were meant to receive. How do you tell the difference between your dreams?

Well, dreams with messages tend to be quite different from a regular dream in regards to their intensity. When you initially awaken, you'll most likely feel as if it was "so real", and maybe it was.

Numbers

Math is a major part of the world that we live in and numbers appear to be another common means of communication with spirit. I spoke at church one Sunday morning and shared my story about Seth and some of the various signs I have received. After the service, a gentleman approached me and said he had a bird that began to appear after he lost his father, very similar to how my cardinal interactions occurred. The gentleman then asked me if numbers ever meant anything to me.

I had not shared the significance of numbers, so his question surprised me. He went on to explain there was a number that meant something special for him and his father, and that particular number had been appearing everywhere he went. I had no doubt it had!

In my case, Seth had been planning to wear the #10 for his first year of t-ball, so that number became very important to us. After his death, everywhere we went, that number seemed to appear. If we went to the movies, it was row x and seat number 10. If we looked at the clock it always seemed to be 10 minutes after the hour. It was constant and caught our attention as we began to notice the pattern.

Another time numbers played a significant moment in our lives was when we traveled to Florida for another vacation. This particular trip included not only myself, Trish, and Alex, but also Heather Deskins and her two daughters, Jordan and Bree. As I mentioned earlier, Heather had lost her husband Bryon, so both of our families were still adjusting to our new lives. Heather rented a large van for the drive, and we all loaded up and headed down south. By the time we finally checked into our hotel in Tampa, we were all exhausted; yet, Jordan noticed immediately the room number we were assigned: 1107.

November 7th was the date Bryon had died, and tucked right there in the middle was Seth's #10. Two families. Two losses. Two numbers that were significant in their meaning for each, combined as one.

They claim spirits like to use numbers that hold some sort of significance to you personally, and the cases I mentioned here certainly seem to back up that theory. So, you'll likely see the same numbers over and over until you get the message, whatever that message may be.

In reality, this makes sense, because, like I mentioned, the world is dominated by mathematics. I could probably write a whole different book on that topic alone, but I'm afraid you'd be too bored to read it so I'll just say mathematics and numbers are an important part of the world we live in, and I'm not surprised signs may come to us in this manner.

Animals

Obviously, I've experienced this phenomena many times, but it's not just birds that may bring a person comfort or a message. Butterflies, dragonflies, and others can all be part of the message world. They claim animals, bird, insects, and more can be used by spirit to communicate with us.

Have you ever had an animal land in front of you? Or did one land directly on you? Maybe they have stared at you through a window or somehow gotten your attention in an unusual way. If it feels like they are trying to get you to pay attention, maybe it's a sign, and you need to actually pay attention!

My wife began to talk to me about a dragonfly that would appear and fly around our house while she was in the back yard during the summer months. It's not surprising they like to hover around the swimming pool, but even when she would sit on the front porch, she seemed to be the one they would come near. Maybe Trish was getting her own sign in this manner. I'll let her make that call, but I wouldn't be surprised in the least.

As for the cardinals, they have moved onto our property now. They actually appear to have formed a nest in the trees to the front of our home and are around constantly these days. We put out a feeder as a little extra motivation to keep them nearby. Their songs still bring us comfort and a sense of peace, and on those difficult days, they always seem to make an appearance.

Small Objects

Objects like coins and feathers are reported as being fairly common as possible signs. They say that small objects may begin to appear everywhere you turn, or maybe just in unusual places. During our trip to Disney World, my wife seemed to find pennies all day long. A friend of ours, Charity Edwards, once shared with me that after losing a loved one in her life, white feathers would show up all over the place. They would appear not only outside by in the house and everywhere else!

Both of these are potential messages a person could be receiving a sign, especially if the object has some type of significance in some way. They claim this is their way of letting you know they're around.

Movement

As I previously mentioned, we have had pictures fall off the wall and we have also had pictures on shelves be turned or out of place. Of course, these things got our attention when they happened, and they claim spirits will move objects to get your attention. Maybe you find things are being moved or always seem to be lost or misplaced. Maybe you're not losing your mind; maybe it's a sign.

Electricity

I shared the story about how our ceiling fan got our attention one day, but our television would turn on during the middle of the night for no reason as well. That happened on a fairly regular basis during the first few months after Seth's death. His toys would also make noises for unexplainable reasons. Initially, all these things freaked us out, but we eventually got used to them. Lately, we don't get those types of signs, but early on it seemed to be very frequent.

They say spirits can absolutely use electricity to communicate with us. This actually makes sense if you think about it, because we are all energy, and energy makes up everything around us. Have you have experienced flickering lights or have you ever had an appliance turning on and/or off for reasons that you cannot explain? Electricity is a conduit, and it may very well be that someone is using it to communicate with you.

Synchronicities

I have actually given several examples of synchronicity throughout this book, but let me give you another one that sums it all up. It was that time of year, and I was once again thinking about my friend Bryon Deskins. I had recently sent a text to his wife, checking in on her and letting her know we were thinking about her and the girls. A day or two later, I was helping a friend DJ a wedding. When he handed me the list of names to announce for the bridal party, I had to smile. The groom that day? Bryan Duskins.

That groom's name is a great example of synchronicity, something that doesn't seem related and yet somehow they still connect with you in a significant way. I'm sure if you think about it, you've experienced synchronicity many times throughout your own life.

My daughter graduated high school, and I had decided I was going to step back from my coaching for a little while, unless a position as a varsity basketball coach opened up. Running a basketball program at the high school level was something I had wanted to try for several years, so I at least wanted to consider that opportunity if one arose.

A position at Fredericktown, a school not far from my home did open up, and after a couple of interviews, I was feeling blessed when I was offered the job. After being hired, one of the first things I wanted to do was watch video from the previous season. Watching the game film would allow me to get a better idea of what the team looked like and I could get a feel for some of the players who would likely be returning.

However, when I logged into the video website to set up an account, I was taken aback by the date that popped up on my screen: March 20, 2013. The day Seth died. For whatever reason, it seemed like I was someplace I was meant to be at that moment. Oh, and the school's mascot? Yeah, it's a cardinal.

Music

On our drive to Florida after the funeral, we experienced certain songs that let us feel our child's presence, and I know many of you have experienced something similar. Music is a great trigger for our memories. Our brains naturally connect certain events and times with the songs we heard during those moments and they claim spirits love to play use that to communicate with us.

There may be times when a random song just pops into your head or on the radio and you have no idea why, but it immediately makes you think of your loved one. Or it may be that you hear a song and know it's your loved one because that particular song meant something of significance.

Sometimes the music is a message for you, and

sometimes it's just letting you know they're still around. It's always comforting to hear those special songs, and it can be even more meaningful when you find yourself singing along with the exact words you needed to hear, right when you needed to heara them.

Feeling Their Presence

I have walked into Seth's room and had this intense feeling he was there. I can't really explain it, and in all fairness, it could have just been all in my mind, but it felt like so much more than that. It would be a different feeling, a chill, this energy I can't really put into words.

They claim this may be a spirit, and you may notice it by an intense feeling that someone's right there next to you. Maybe you felt that tingle or you got that "cold chill." I think most all of us have had that at some point in our lives. Maybe it was your loved one. Mabye it was something else, but be aware and watch for those moments. You just never know!

Thoughts

If you ever suddenly think of something that seems to be out of the blue, it could be a message for you. For example, let's say you suddenly have an urge to go to the park and you just aren't sure why. Then while at the park, you see a certain flower that reminds you of your loved one.

It's very possible you were meant to go to that park that day so a message could be delivered to you. Anytime an idea just unexpectedly pops into your mind or you're suddenly inspired to do something specific, you could be being led for some reason. Maybe you need to just go with whatever that thought is and see where it leads you.

I initially had no intention of writing a children's book, but I kept getting this thought about doing exactly that. Something just kept saying to me, *That Snuggle Time story sure would make a great children's book, and it could make a big difference for some people.*

I ignored that thought initially, but it kept repeating, then people on social media began telling me the same thing. Finally, I relented and went for it. Someone knew someone who knew someone, and suddenly I had an editor in California with 30+ years of experience who brought my story to life. She then connected me with a professional illustrator in Indonesia to do the pictures, and before long Seth's Snuggle Time Game was a reality.

We have never marketed the book on a major scale or anything, choosing instead to share it with family, friends, and our Facebook followers, yet somehow we have managed to move more than 1,500 of those books, and it's more than paid for itself already. We've received emails from people all over, telling us how much the book means to them and how impactful it is.

The point is, all of that happened as a result of a thought that seemed to come from somewhere other than inside myself. I suppose it could be my subconscious coming to the forefront, but then again it could be yet another sign. It's another one of those things that I'm not going to spend too much time overthinking. Instead I'm just going to enjoy the moment!

Clairaudience

They say there are times when you can literally hear the voice of your deceased loved one. They even have a name for it: Clairaudience. Internal clairaudience is the most common way to hear a voice, because it's easier for spirit to speak to you through your thoughts and mind.

A great example of this could be how, when I was interacting with the cardinal, I heard a voice inside my head directing me to "look down." They would certainly label that as internal clairaudience. However, my entire family has experienced the external version of this as well.

One day my daughter texted me at work, because she claimed to have heard Seth call out her name one morning before school and it really freaked her out. When I told my wife what Allie had experienced, she proceeded to tell me she had heard him call out a few times as well.

I took it all with a grain of salt, because hearing a voice calling out seemed like a lot more than most of the other things we had experienced. However, a few days later I was at home alone, watching television in the family room, and I heard what sounded like someone talking. I muted the television and heard the noise even more clearly. I assumed it was my daughter or wife and I just had not realized they were home already. I walked down the hallway towards Seth's room and froze dead in my tracks.

"Mom. Mom," was what I heard. It was as clear as day, and I had no doubt whose voice it was I was hearing.

A shiver shot down my spine, and I called out, "Seth?" as I walked into his room. The voice stopped, and I was met with nothing but silence from that moment on.

I decided I wasn't even going to try to explain it, so I was glad to learn they have a name for it, clairaudience. I really thought I was losing it that day! My wife and daughter claimed that happened to them several times as time went on, as for me it has never happened again.

Final Thoughts On Signs

I have listed several possible signs here that I have had some level of personal experience with, but there are many others as well. If you have not experienced any of these, it may be that you just have yet to recognize them. I firmly believe all of us get them at some point in our life. You are just as special as I am, or as any of us are, so keep watching!

I have been told the better you are doing, the less likely it is you will receive a sign. However, if you keep your mind open and stay observant, you will eventually likely receive a message. For me, it seems like every time I am feeling down or out of sorts, the cardinal comes. As I sit here today, writing this very section, I can hear the cardinal outside singing his song. Maybe that is not exactly a sign in the traditional sense, but it feels so good to still hear.

One last thought: Please remember that our loved ones now live in a better place. Their sicknesses, ailments, and problems are all over. They have left all those things behind. I was once told that maybe we are looking at it all wrong. Our loved ones just went home, where they truly belong. The rest of us are still on an extended vacation here on Earth; one day our trip will be over and we will be heading home too, so the separation is only temporary.

CHAPTER TWENTY-FOUR

Consciousness

C oming to terms that somehow signs may actually be possible left me with many unanswered questions so I continued searching. In 2017 I came across an article by Arjun Walia entitled, "When You Die, You Might Know That You're Dead, Scientists Discover Signs of Life After Death."

The article was very well-written and I found the topic of consciousness intriguing. What happens to our consciousness after we die? Does it just cease to exist or does it somehow live on? If consciousness is simply a product of the brain then it must stop when the brain dies, right? Unfortunately, Science has never had a tool or the ability to measure something like this so these questions couldn't previously be answered, but things are beginning to change as technology evolves.

In his article, Arjun discusses a study by a team from New York University's Lagone School of Medicine. He states, "They actually investigated twin studies from Europe and the United States that looked at people who suffered cardiac arrest, flat-lined, and then came back to life. We're talking about people whose hearts have stopped; once this happens, blood no longer circulates to the brain, which means brain function is also completely dead."

Arjun goes on to explain that "The study was the largest of its kind and involved 2,060 patients from 15 different hospitals in the United Kingdom, United States, and Austria. The study found, as have several others, that many of these patients were still aware and able to see following their biological death, but from "outside" their body, so to speak. The portion of the study that focused on UK cases, which was conducted over a four year period found that nearly 40% of people who survived described some type of 'awareness' during the time they were pronounced clinically dead, before their hearts were restarted."

Fascinating, isn't it? How could so many patients experience awareness during death if something extraordinary weren't going on? Either these people are experiencing something truly phenomenal, and consciousness does continue on after death, or there must be slight brain activity still going on and that is what is creating the experience.

The latter is harder to believe, given the fact that if there is any brain activity happening beyond our ability to detect it, it has to be extremely minuscule. So how could such minimal brain activity provide such an expansive experience?

The idea that consciousness continues after death certainly seems a more logical conclusion. Many scientists within the areas of neuroscience and even quantum physics will say that consciousness is the backbone of physical material matter because it is *required* to create physical matter.

I want to thank Arjun for allowing me to reference so much of his article for this chapter of the book. His entire premise made me think back to a podcast interview I did with Sherman O'Bryan about one year ago. Sherman's story essentially backs up what Arjun was arguing.

Sherman is a father of ten children, a grandfather, and a veteran of twenty-two years. He was always an extremely active guy who enjoyed working with his hands, building and fixing things. He also spent much of his time umpiring youth baseball games and supporting his local community. On weekends Sherman would bartend, enjoying the social lifestyle that the job would bring.

However, in 2004 all of that changed dramatically when Sherman became sick. Within three months of becoming ill, he ended up confined to a hospital bed, where he would spend the next several years of his life. Sherman was eventually diagnosed with Sarcoidosis, a neurological disease affecting several organs. When combined with other afflictions he was suffering from, it all rendered him unable to function as he once had. Sherman would never again be able to bartend, umpire, or do many of the other things that he loved. Needless to say that affected his mindset greatly.

"I was angry at God. I was angry at my family. I was angry at everything," Sherman said. He became extremely depressed and basically began to give up. His passion to live was gone. Why fight against something that has taken away so much of who you are? Is there a reason to try? These are common thoughts when life comes at you in unexpected ways, ways that leave you questioning everything that you thought you knew. Sherman fell into that trap and the depression simply took over.

As time continued to tick off the clock-of-life, Sherman realized he was simply wasting away. The world was passing him by as he sat there, doing nothing. So one night he gave in and began to pray. It had been a long time since he had the strength, or willingness, to talk to God but he knew that was where he had to turn.

As he prayed, Sherman kept it simply, asking God for guidance and help. He was finally ready to battle again.

"It was family that gave me hope. Family is everything. I had to do something," he said.

Before long, Sherman was out of that hospital bed that had been his home for so long. He was using braces and assistance devices to move around. He was taking the recommended medications. He was starting to take his life back.

Things weren't easy, but at least he wasn't stuck in bed anymore. Life was different, but he was living again. Then one day something happened that changed the entire game and altered Sherman's state of mind forever.

In the interview Sherman stated, "It was in February of 2008, I remember it very vividly. My family and I were sitting out on the front porch and I was on the swing when suddenly I went into a seizure. I died that day. Now during this period of time, my son was giving me CPR. They were trying to work on me to get me back and this entire time I was standing there watching it all. I had what they refer to as an out-of-body experience.

"I watched as my family called 9-1-1. I saw the squad arrive and I watched as the EMTs worked on me. They eventually loaded me into the squad and took me to the local hospital. It seemed like they were stabilizing me several times, but every time that I thought it was working they would lose me again. I watched all of this, including in the ER, that day and it was surreal to say the least.

"My view was from above and I was thinking, is that really me on the table? It can't be. Things around me seemed really bright and I didn't really know where I was at. I'm not sure if it was disorientation or what you'd call it, but I just recall how bright everything seemed. I had no pain at that time. In fact, I felt really good. I thought how healthy I seemed finally, but at the same time I was looking down at my body lying there. It was an unbelievable thing to experience.

"Finally, they were able to get my body working again and the next thing I realized I was in a hospital bed. I opened my eyes to see my wife there in the room with me. She wanted to tell me what had happened, but I stopped her. I then proceeded to tell her about my own experience and what had occurred.

"To say there is not a God doesn't make sense, because I know differently. When I was in that state I thought it was really over, but somebody or something touched me on the shoulder. I heard a voice telling me that it wasn't my time yet and that I still had things to do. So today I'm alive and able to share this story. I still get goosebumps whenever I talk about it. It was literally unbelievable and I've had people not believe me when I tell them what happened. They don't have to believe it though. It was something that I experienced and it changed me. That's enough for me.

"Don't every say that there's not a God or not a Heaven. I saw it. Well, I didn't actually see God, but I know in my heart that it's all real. I felt it. There's something more out there and it's waiting for all of us. We'll get there, but not until it's our time."

So does consciousness live on? It sure seems like there's a strong case. A very strong case.

If you are of the Christian faith and believe in God and an afterlife then maybe you already believe; maybe you already have no doubt that consciousness lives on. If you are a Buddhist then you absolutely believe that consciousness lives after death. However, if your faith has been tested and you just aren't sure anymore, I hope that this chapter gives you something a little more concrete than just blind faith, although faith is the key, and it always will be.

Romans 1:17 (KJV)
"For therein is the righteousness of God revealed from faith to faith; as it is written, the just shall live by faith."

CHAPTER TWENTY-FIVE

How To Talk About Loss

There are many times when we face a situation where someone we know loses a loved one and we are not sure what to say. What we typically end up doing is repeating one of the common phrases we have heard in our lifetime, yet that may not be the right thing at all.

When someone we know loses a loved one many of us are unsure about how to handle that.

What should I do? Should I send a card? Should I send flowers? Should I make a phone call? Should I stop by and visit?

What exactly do you do in these types of situations? I'm guessing many of us say or do many of the same things. I'm also guessing many of us approach these situations differently than others. So is there a right way or a wrong way?

These questions led me to reminisce about the many things others said or did for us after Seth passed. Every single one of them meant well, and they were definitely trying to show their support. However, not every statement made me feel better at that particular point in time.

So, first let's take a look at some of the things people said that didn't really help. Again, I know these comments were meant to be a show of support, but in my case they certainly weren't helpful, at least not right after I experienced losing my child.

Author Note: My responses to these statements were originally written at a time when the pain was still very fresh and so I may or may not feel quite the same way now.

1. "*It gets easier with time.*" As I write this, it isn't any easier. I feel like this is just one big lie. Maybe they're right, but right now it's now what I need to hear.

2. "*Anything you need, just let me know.*" Thanks, but the one thing I need, you

can't give me. I actually have mixed emotions about this statement. On the one hand, it's nice to know they offered, but at the same time, I'm not in a place where I know what I want, so I'm not likely to ask.

3. *"Stay strong."* I want to be strong, and I may even be seen as strong by others, but I'm weak, so very weak. Inside, I just can't be anything else. Why would we expect anyone to be strong during times like this?

4. *"I know how you feel."* If you lost your child, then maybe you do. If you haven't, then there's no way you can. Actually, I hope you don't.

5. *"He's in a better place now."* Maybe, but here I am. He may be there, but I'm stuck here – without him. I didn't find this statement to be comforting in any way. I already knew he moved on to a better place, but that didn't stop the pain or make it alright. As I gain more distance from the event though, it's somewhat reassuring. It just wasn't in those early days.

6. *"God needed an angel."* Maybe, but I needed my child. He completed me. God knew that, didn't he?

There are several more statements and comments that I could list, but you get the idea. As I stated earlier, all the things listed here are well-meaning, but they hurt me when I initially heard them. These days, I wouldn't necessarily take them the same way, but in the immediate aftermath of tragedy, your mind doesn't process things the way you might later.

As humans, we have a desire to find just the right words. We truly want to give others who are suffering strength and hope. It is totally natural to try to find something to say, but the truth is, there is no poem, phrase, or words that can help in the way you would hope.

So, let's move on to things that did help. What things do I remember the most? What meant something? Well, let me give you a few of the things that stood out to me during those early days, in no particular order:

1. The Expressions of Caring. It didn't matter whether it was a sympathy card, flowers, a phone call, a donation of some type, or if it came in some other form. Just the fact that we knew that others genuinely cared about what we were going through helped

more than I can explain. It wasn't what they said, but the fact that they just cared. Even the statements I mentioned earlier, although maybe not the best, still showed the effort.

2. The Food. I never realized how important having food so readily available during times like that was. I'll never forget Cathy Brake, among others, who provided food for us those first several days. Her pies were simply some of the best I've ever had. I'll forever be grateful for her, but there were certainly many others as well, including the local church ladies who ensured that we had enough to eat the day of the funeral. No one went hungry, that was for certain! Of course, it was still difficult to eat, and my wife barely touched any of the food, but just having it right there waiting if needed really did help, and it was certainly appreciated. It was another expression of caring, one that's always well-received.

3. Family and Friends Just Being There. I couldn't possibly list all the family and friends who stood beside us during those early days, but let me assure you, in your darkest hour you'll

find out who the truly good people are. We're extremely blessed to have an amazing family, and many incredible friends as well. They truly gave me strength just by being there. That matters more than I can explain. To this day I still remember my brother Kevin and cousin Tubby standing by my side during the showing. And just standing there was enough.

4. In Memory Of – There were softball and soccer games in Seth's memory, a beautiful concrete bench was made with Seth's name engraved on it, and the local youth baseball board even named the t-ball field after him. There was a poker run. The kids at school organized events and ways to remember Seth. Businesses donated things, and people helped remodel our home. The list goes on and on. They all cared. One of the things you don't want is for other to forget your loved one so the memorial things can certainly have a lasting effect.

At the end of the day, we've been able to think about our son in a positive way by seeing how others have reacted in his memory. Knowing he is remembered, and will be, is truly special, and it helps so much.

I would encourage you just to remember that the words we try to use in difficult times do not always help, but our actions can make a real difference. When those actions come from a place of love, when they show your support, and when they let others know you truly care, it will always work.

So, the next time something happens around you and you are not sure how to react, try to remember these things. I assure you, you will make a bigger impact and be remembered in the way we all want to be. You will be remembered as a good friend, and as a good person while providing the kind of comfort that someone needs at that exact moment in time.

CHAPTER TWENTY-SIX

You Are Not Alone

I wrote this and originally posted it on Seth's Facebook page in January of 2014 while reflecting on what we had gone through up to that point in time. I have decided to include it in this book in the hope that it may help someone who needs to know that they really are not alone.

YOU ARE NOT ALONE

I celebrated a birthday this week. I'd like to say it was a wonderful day, but like most days, things still aren't the same since the accident. It seems like every time you think you're moving on or are feeling better, something comes along and smacks you right in the face, and suddenly you're right back there, feeling that pain and despair all over again. I'm not writing this for sympathy or to garner attention, but rather to let others who are out there feeling this way to know YOU ARE NOT ALONE.

During the day I work in management, in the evening I coach in the local school system. I'm a fairly normal, everyday kind of guy, but I have to admit, it seems like every so often I turn into an emotional wreck. I'm not the guy I normally am when those moments hit. These days, I've figured out how to hide it from others pretty well. Everyone thinks you're doing OK because you smile and laugh publicly. You learn what triggers your moments and so you try to avoid them the best you can. You take deep breaths and walk away when the need arises. I was told it gets easier, but I'm not so sure. I think you just learn how to hide it, adjust to it, and live with it; however, 'easier' isn't a term I would use. Still, just know that YOU ARE NOT ALONE.

Yesterday, while sitting at my desk in the office, I heard a siren in the distance. I live just a few miles from where I work, and the day Seth died, I also heard those sirens. As the sirens got closer, it triggered that day all over again in my mind. Tears filled my eyes, it became hard to breathe, and the events of March 20, 2013 flooded my thoughts and overtook everything I was doing. For the next five minutes, I sat in a trance, unable to do much of anything except sit there and wait for the moment to pass. Eventually it did, and I was able to turn my attention back to the work at hand.

A lot of people call me strong, but moments like those make you feel like the weakest person in the world. However, I'm coming to realize it's OK. It's natural. It's expected. If you're suffering and have one of those moments - know that YOU ARE NOT ALONE.

Some nights, you may find it hard to sleep. You stay up late watching television shows you don't care about or maybe you sit and read a book. Maybe you surf the internet. There are a hundred different things you may do to pass the time. Sometimes sleep is hard to find. I always think of an old Garth Brooks' song that says, "I used to sit and talk to you - they're all just a substitute - to get through one night a day." It's a pretty accurate description of how the night can be the worst. It's quiet, and the silence can be reflective, but it can also consume you when your heart is heavy, but know that YOU ARE NOT ALONE.

Lately, one of my favorite things to do is sit and look at old pictures. It somehow feels so good just to see his little five-year-old face. Seth always seemed to be happy, and even now when I look at the pictures, I realize he really was a very happy kid, full of energy and love. That smile lit up a room, and it still does in those pictures. The majority of days, those pictures bring a smile to my face. Other days, they bring tears to my eyes. The pictures can bring me such joy and pain at the same time, but I'm glad I have them. If this is the way you feel, know that YOU ARE NOT ALONE.

I could go on, but just know that you are not alone. Millions of people out there have suffered before we did. Many are suffering right now, and unfortunately, many more will face this pain in the near future. For those of you who believe, you know God suffered as well. He knows the pain and what we are going through. So, let me end by saying even though our natural human nature is to cry and suffer, we should find some comfort in knowing our loved ones are in a better place than we are and THEY ARE NOT ALONE.

CHAPTER TWENTY-SEVEN

I've Learned Stuff

Originally written as a Facebook post on another birthday of Seth's, I felt that this was something that was truly worth sharing.

Facebook Post on November 14, 2016

As we celebrate yet another birthday without our son, I reflect on the journey so far without him. It certainly has not been easy, and along the way I've learned a lot. So, in honor of his birthday, and in Seth's memory, I give you things I've learned since losing my child.

I've learned in tragic moments, the human spirit can rise above the ugliness and show amazing love for one another. After Seth's death, I witnessed others give their time, support, love, money, food, and more. I watched as an entire community gave support and comfort to a family in need. I can never express how much those things meant just when we needed it most, but I know the human spirit around the world rises up for others when it is needed the most, and it is one of the most beautiful things when it occurs. It truly gives you hope in a world that sometimes seems hopeless.

I've learned the true meaning of life has nothing to do with money and everything to do with love. No matter how rich you are (or aren't), it means nothing if you don't have those relationships with others. When you learn how to love, truly and deeply, you are rich beyond all else. It really is that simple. Congratulations – you now know the true meaning of life!

We make it so complicated, but the truth is – there's nothing complicated about it. The King James Version of the Bible has several verses that emphasize this point. 1 John 4:12 states *"No man hath seen God at any time. If we love one another, God dwelleth in us, and his love is perfected in us"* while Galatians 5:14 sums it up with *"For all the law is fulfilled in one word, even this; Thou shalt love thy neighbor as thyself."*

I've learned that I don't know nearly as much as I thought I did. We all get caught up in what we think we know, yet there is so much more to learn. After losing Seth, I was able to open my eyes to the beauty of nature, to witness the true beauty of what's been created. I saw the signs. I was able to open my mind to learning new things. I was able to open myself to new experiences. I took chances. I'm not the same person I was before my child died, but maybe that's a good thing. Now I'm willing to learn, willing to grow, willing to live outside of my comfort zone - because I've been living there since the day he left.

I've learned I'm powerful beyond measure. All of us are. I never dreamt I would write a book. It never even crossed my mind, yet after Seth's death, it happened. I never pictured myself as making a difference in the world in any profound way, not really. I'm just an average guy, living an average life in a small one-stoplight town in Ohio. I'm no more special than you or anyone else, yet I've come to understand that we're all *very* special.

We all can make a difference if we choose to be passionate about something. If we are motivated and passionate about something, anything, then we can make a real difference. I have no doubt about that statement, because we are all powerful beyond measure.

I've learned the pain never goes away. I'm sorry if you've recently lost someone. You undoubtedly will hear that it will "get better with time," but the truth is – it may not. Life will go on. New experiences will be had. You will learn how to cope without feeling like it's all over, but the pain will always be there. It's called love, and love never ends - not if it was true and unconditional.

But guess what? That's OK. It doesn't have to stop you from living a full life. It will just be a different life than what it was. That's reality. It won't necessarily be easy. Don't let it consume you, but know that it's OK for it to exist regardless of what others may say. And know that one day you'll understand why it happened the way it did. That day may not be today or tomorrow, but one day.

So love, live life, and be happy. I know that's hard to do at times, but it's how we make the most out of what we have left.

CHAPTER TWENTY-EIGHT

Five Things My Five-Year-Old Taught Me

Having kids taught me many things in life. Quite honestly, it changed my entire outlook in ways I would never have imagined. However, in March of 2013 when my son died, I learned things I did not want to know, but I have also been thinking about what an amazing impact he had while he was here with us. So, here is my list of the five things my five-year-old taught me:

<u>#1: Everybody deserves to be loved</u>.

Seth gave out more love in five years than most of us do in an entire lifetime. Sometimes as adults, we tend to hold grudges, stick to our inner circles, and basically forget we were meant to love one another (not just those close to us). Many times, we don't even think about loving those we don't know, but with Seth, he gave love constantly and got loved back in return. He never met someone he didn't show kindness towards, and he exuded love. His life was rich beyond measure in that way. How much better would the world be if we all could remember to do that on a daily basis?

#2: Hugs = Happiness.

Sure, this falls under the guise of love, but in Seth's little world, giving and getting hugs were the "coolest" thing ever, and he gave them out constantly. I cannot tell you how many times I watched someone's face light up when Seth embraced them with one of his hugs. I know my own world would light up the moment his little arms wrapped around me and gave me a big hug and I heard, "I love you, Daddy."

#3: It's OK to be direct.

Seth liked to try and help me coach my daughter's basketball team when she was in Junior High, and many times he would correct the girls if he thought they were doing something wrong. He didn't mince words or try to sugarcoat how he felt. It was basically, "You need to do it like this because that's not right." Straightforward and to the point. He was never mean or judging in any way. It was just matter-of-factly "Get it right." As kids we tend to be that way, but as we grow older we seem to lose that special gift. So, be honest – but do it without passing judgment.

#4: Spend time with those you love.

Seth and I had our nightly Snuggle Time ritual, but we also played outdoors together, and many times when I got home from work, I would get down on the floor and play cars with him (after he begged repeatedly). Seth loved spending time with me, but also with his mom, sister, grandma, and others. He truly enjoyed his family time and time with friends. Sometimes we all get so busy in this hectic world, we miss those special moments. No one is promised tomorrow, so we need to live in the here and now while we can.

#5: Try something new, you might like it.

Seth was terrified by the idea of jumping into the swimming pool and going under water. For whatever reason, it simply scared him, but eventually he trusted me enough to let me stand in the pool and catch him. After much debate, he finally jumped in, and I caught him before he went under – then I surprised him and went under with him. After we emerged, he coughed up a little water, then his eyes lit up and I knew what was next.

I ended up spending the next hour catching my son as he backed up, ran to the edge, and jumped in as far as he could, laughing, yelling, and making sure everyone saw him. He had the time of his life! Sometimes we think something is so scary in life, but maybe – just maybe – if we're willing to take that leap, it might just turn out to be the most exhilarating moment ever (and it doesn't hurt if you take that leap with someone you trust by your side).

Conclusion

I hope you have enjoyed reading *When the Cardinal Calls*, and I want to thank you for taking the time to go on this journey with me. It's been quite a ride so far, and it's not done yet. I plan to continue to share my experiences, and I hope you continue to follow along.

One place you will be able to find me is on the website: www.whenthecardinalcalls.com. There, you will find my blog and additional articles, along with the *When the Cardinal Calls* podcast, special videos, featured pictures, and additional book information. If you take the time to sign up on the site then you will even have access to a special bonus book chapter on bunk bed safety. It's a pretty intense chapter and it also provides some interesting information about bunk bed safety that you will definitely want to check out. The chapter was originally included in this book, but cut during editing. However, I'm not sure that it should have been.

On the site, you will also be able to share *your* amazing story and potentially be featured in an article. Who knows, your story may actually be put into a future book. I've shared my story and now I want to share yours! Every single one of us has a story to tell - so tell it.

Email us on the site www.whenthecardinalcalls.com with your tales of loss, talk to us about the signs you have received, and/or let us know how you managed to overcome adversity in your life. We want to hear all about it.

Finally, please be sure to leave a book review online wherever you have the opportunity to do so. Book reviews are a big help to authors like myself who do not have a major publishing agency behind them. We have to do all of our own marketing and your reviews will help let others know if picking up a copy of this book is valuable or not. Obviously, I hope that you think it was!

I also hope this book has allowed you to find some level of comfort and it generates some truly open-minded discussions about the concept of signs, the world that we currently live in, and the one that awaits us all in the future.

"Loss is only a temporary separation."

Special Acknowledgement

A special thank you to my wife, Trish Maceyko, and my daughter, Allie Maceyko, both whom gave up countless hours of time that we could have spent together so that I could write this book. Like anything in life you have to give up something when you want something and so I appreciate the fact that they supported me during a process that spanned several years. I cannot adequately express my gratitude for their being there.

And to my mom, Betty Maceyko, who took us in when things went so horribly wrong, and has suffered alongside us these last several years. A mother's love is never-ending and amazes me.

43325250R00116

Made in the USA
Middletown, DE
22 April 2019